Inside Anne Frank's House
An Illustrated Journey through Anne's World

Inside Anne Frank's House

An Illustrated Journey through Anne's World

Introduction by Hans Westra,
Executive Director, Anne Frank House

OVERLOOK DUCKWORTH
Woodstock • New York • London

"One day this terrible war will be over.
The time will come when we will be people
again and not just Jews!"
"We can never be just Dutch, or just English,
or whatever, we will always be Jews as well.
But then, we'll want to be."

Anne Frank, April 9, 1944

"One day this terrible war will be over. The time will come when we will be people again and not just Jews," writes Anne Frank in her diary on April 9, 1944. At that moment around 100,000 of the 140,000 Jewish residents of the Netherlands have been deported to concentration and extermination camps. Around 25,000 Jews have gone into hiding to avoid this fate; 17,000 of them will survive the war.

The group of eight people in hiding, which included Anne, is betrayed. On September 3, 1944 they are placed on the last train leaving Westerbork transit camp headed for Auschwitz. We know that Anne died in Bergen-Belsen concentration camp in March 1945. Just a few weeks later, on April 15th, the English army liberated the camp. Of the people in hiding only Otto Frank returned after the war. He arranged the 1947 publication of Anne's diary. To date her book has been translated into approximately sixty languages.

The diary of Anne Frank ends on August 1, 1944. She left no accounting of her experiences in the German *SD*-prison in Amsterdam or of her journey through the camps Westerbork, Auschwitz, and Bergen-Belsen. Still her diary is for many of its readers a first acquaintance with this period of history. To many others, Anne Frank has become the "face" of the millions of victims of the Shoah. The writer Primo Levi, who survived Auschwitz, explained this as follows: "One single Anne Frank moves us more than the countless others who suffered just as she did but whose faces have remained in the shadows. Perhaps it is better that way; if we were capable of taking in all the suffering of all those people, we would not be able to live."

By reading Anne Frank's book one is personally confronted with the reality of the persecution of the Jews. It is therefore understandable that many people want to see the actual hiding place where Anne wrote her diary. Over the course of the years this interest has continued to grow, giving rise to a paradoxical situation in which hundreds of thousands of people per year want to visit one of Amsterdam's most hidden and secretive places.

The Anne Frank House opened in 1960 as a small museum. To welcome visitors, the front part of the building – the former business premises – was rebuilt as a reception and exhibition space. Only the back part of the house, also known as the annex, was left in its authentic state. Between 1996 and 1999, a new building was constructed next to the two canal-side houses that until that moment were the museum's home. This facilitated returning the front part of the house to the way it was during the hiding period. This section located in the front of the building played an important role in the story of the hiding period. Once the warehouse workers downstairs had gone home, the people in hiding could come out of the Secret Annex and spend time in the work spaces and the offices of Otto Frank's company.

Visitors to 263 Prinsengracht are taken on a journey back in time. In each of the rooms, excerpts from Anne's diary provide an impression of what happened there during the hiding period. Visitors encounter traces of the inhabitants of the Secret Annex, but also of the four employees of Otto Frank who did so much to help the people in hiding.

In compiling this book, we followed the museum-route through the Anne Frank House. The quotations and objects displayed in the actual exhibition can also be found here, supplemented by background information. After the arrest on August 4, 1944, the Secret Annex was emptied of all its furnishings by order of the German Occupation authorities. To provide a better impression of the situation during the hiding period, color photographs of a temporary refurnishing of both the front part of the house and the Secret Annex, are included in this book. In 1954, black & white photographs of the Anne Frank House were made by the photographer Maria Austria. Many of these photographs also appear here.

"We can never be just Dutch, or just English, or whatever, we will always be Jews as well. But then, we'll want to be," wrote Anne on April 9, 1944. Today people are still being persecuted and murdered because they, just like Anne, are not only "different" but also "want to be". This makes a visit to the Anne Frank House meaningful, also in our times.

Hans Westra

Executive Director, Anne Frank House

A Prior History

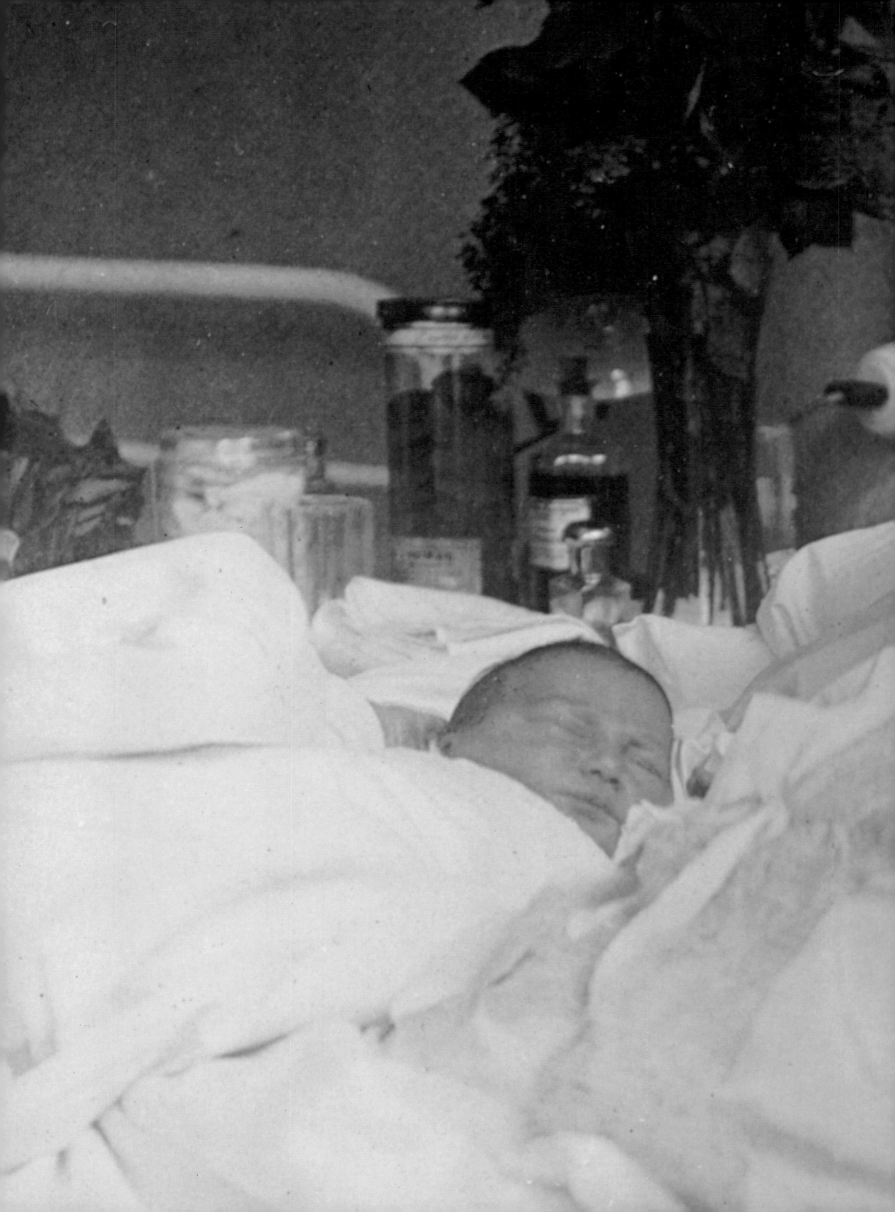

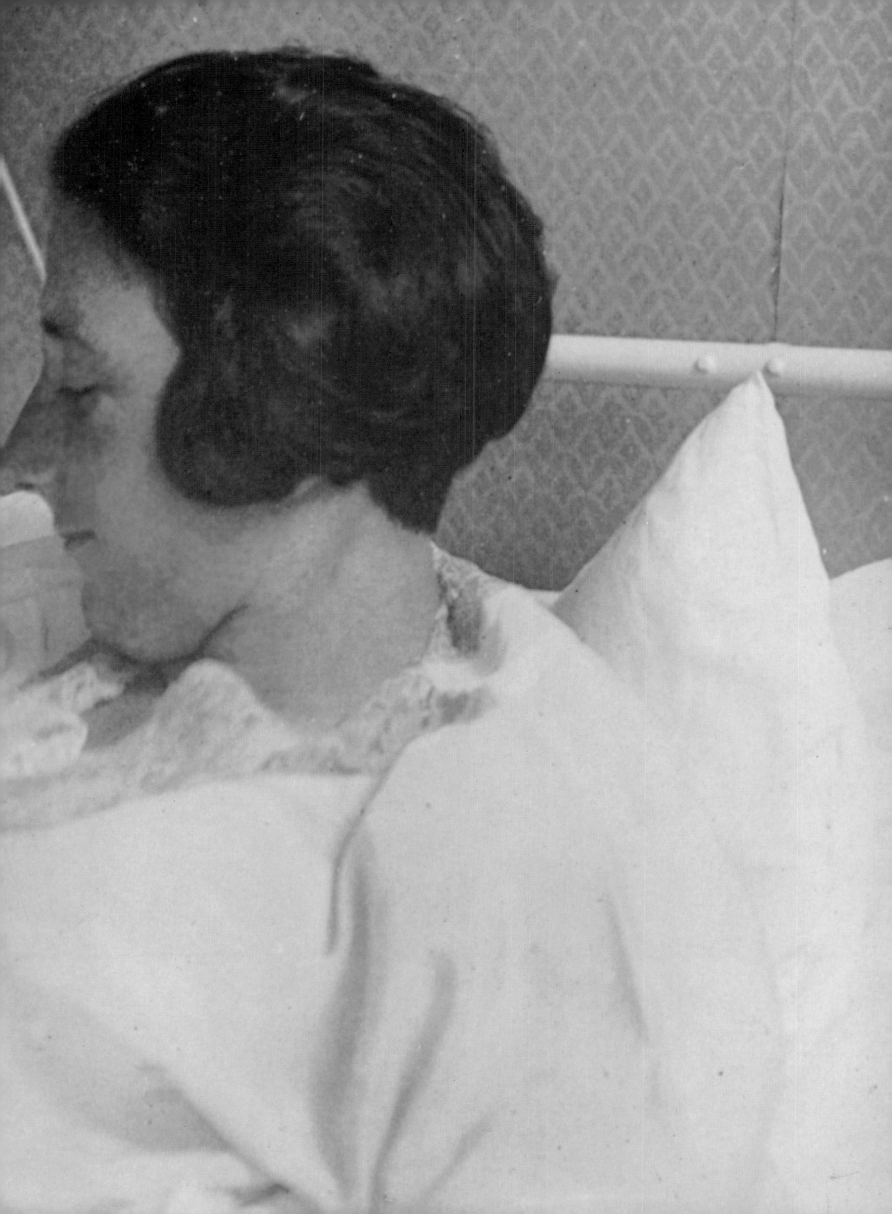

"My father, the most precious father I've ever seen, didn't marry my mother until he was thirty-six and she was twenty-five. My sister Margot was born in 1926 in Frankfurt am Main in Germany. I followed on June 12, 1929." (Anne Frank)

Otto Frank and Edith Holländer are married on May 12, 1925, Otto's birthday. The marriage takes place in the synagogue in Aachen. Nine months later, on February 16, 1926, their first daughter Margot Betti is born. Anne(lies) Marie follows on June 12, 1929. The Franks are secular Jews. Anne's parents feel connected with the Jewish faith yet are not strictly religious. Edith visits the synagogue regularly.

Edith's ancestors emigrate from the Netherlands to Germany at the end of the 18th century and it is due to this that the family carries the name "Holländer". Edith's father manages a business dealing in used iron and metal. Edith, the youngest, is born on January 16, 1900. Her brother Julius is then five years old, Walter is two and her sister Betti is one. Betti dies of appendicitis at the age of sixteen. In 1916, Edith passes her final exams from the Victoria-School, a private Protestant girls' high school in Aachen.

The ancestors of Otto's mother have been in Frankfurt am Main since the 17th century. Otto's father Michael owns a bank and a company that sells throat lozenges. He and his wife Alice have four children: Robert (b. 1886), Otto (b. 1889), Herbert (b. 1891), and Helene (b. 1893). Following high school Otto studies economics in Heidelberg but he quickly cuts short his studies. After a year of training at a bank in Frankfurt, he goes to New York for two years and does internships at Macy's Department Store and in banking. Otto returns to Germany in 1911 and works for an industrial concern in Düsseldorf.

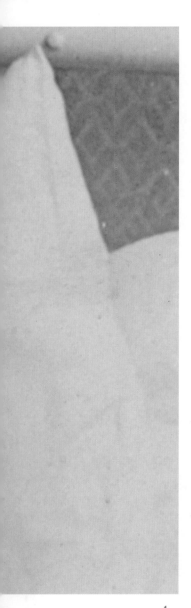

1 2   3

← Anne Frank and her mother, one day after Anne's birth.
2 Edith Holländer, circa 1920.
3 Otto Frank and Edith Frank-Holländer on their honeymoon in San Remo (Italy), 1925.

Edith Frank-
Holländer in 1928

"Anne does so many silly things."

Edith keeps a baby book for Anne, as she did for Margot. She writes about Margot extensively, the entries about her second daughter are limited to catchwords. Among the things that Edith notes about Anne's first months are the following: "Annelies Marie, born on June 12, 1929, 7:30 a.m., 8 1/4 pounds, 21 1/4 inches. Mother and Margot visit the baby sister on June 14th. Margot is completely delighted. Home on June 24th. At night for six weeks she cries a lot. Julius and Walter arrive by car on July 6th. Anne is suffering from the heat wave. A few tears on July 14th, smiles at papa on July 22nd. We travel with Anne to Aachen on August 10th, she cries a lot during the trip, finally calms down in the car, begins crying again in Aachen. She gets better and better, before long drinks two and then three bottles per day. She's content if someone, mainly Uncle Julius, comes into her room in the morning and she does so many silly things. We return home on September 3rd. Anne sleeps all the way."

The main synagogue and the weekly market in Frankfurt am Main in 1927. The Jewish community is primarily concentrated in larger cities like Frankfurt and Berlin. Somewhat more than half-a-million Jews live in Germany in 1925, less than one percent of the population.

A Jewish (kosher) butcher's shop in Berlin, 1931. At the end of the nineteenth century, after centuries of discrimination, Jews received equal rights also in Germany.

Otto Frank in 1915

First Returned the Horses to their Rightful Owners
In later years, Otto Frank does not talk much about his experiences during World War One. He was a member of an artillery regiment. In November 1917, his regiment is involved in the first great tank battle in history near Cambrai (Northern France). A year later a cease-fire is declared. Otto Frank experiences the war as "debilitating". "Only the past," he writes to his mother, "clears the mind." The letters to his sister Helene are fatherly, he is aware of her concerns and gives her good advice. Looking back, Otto Frank says about his superior: "(He) was a democratic man who didn't allow an officer's mess or mess hall servants in his squad. When I was a lieutenant myself, I tried to deal with my men in the same way." Otto doesn't encounter actual anti-Semitism in the army. Shortly after World War One ends, Robert and Herbert, the brothers of Otto, return home. The family anxiously awaits the arrival of their other son. After two months, Otto finally comes home. His parents are amazed when they hear the reason for the delay: Otto has first returned the horses appropriated by his army unit to their rightful owners.

German Jewish soldiers observing Yom Kippur in the synagogue in Brussels (Belgium), 1915. Many Jews feel committed to their country: during World War One – 100,000 Jews fight for Germany, 12,000 die in battle, 30,000 are decorated, 19,000 are promoted of whom 2,000 become officers.

"I wouldn't go as far as to say that I did not feel like a Jew then. Yet, in one way or another, I was consciously aware of being a German. Otherwise, I certainly wouldn't have become an officer in World War One and I wouldn't have fought for Germany." (Otto Frank)

Otto Frank identifies with being German and fights for Germany in World War One (1914-1918), as do his brothers Herbert and Robert. Otto is decorated and promoted to the rank of officer. During World War One, his mother works as a volunteer in a military hospital. Also the oldest brother of Edith, Julius Holländer, serves in the German army. He is shot in the arm during the war and is left with a stiff elbow. After the war Otto Frank, together with his younger brother Herbert, manages the family-owned bank and the trade in throat lozenges.

Germany loses World War One. The Peace Treaty of Versailles (1919) requires Germany to pay massive war reparations. The country plunges into an economic and political crisis. Many people are looking for a scapegoat and blame the Jewish community in Germany for the political and economic malaise. Despite much assimilation there is still evidence of anti-Semitism that manifests itself, especially in this time of crisis.

Even with the large scale economic problems, widespread poverty, and the anti-Semitism, a very liberal atmosphere prevails in Germany – if only in the larger cities. Following World War One, Germany receives its first democratic constitution that is drawn up in Weimar. These years of the "Weimar Republic" will go down in history as the *"Goldenen Zwanziger"* ('Golden Twenties').

6

By around 1923, Germany's inflation has reached a record high and the currency no longer has any value. Affixed to this postcard sent to the Netherlands is 2.5 billion marks in stamps. The sender writes on the reverse side: "I believe I've put enough stamps on this; the financial situation is an absolute chaos."

4 Otto Frank as an officer, 1918.
5 Alice Frank-Stern, the mother of Otto Frank, as a hospital volunteer, 1916.
6 Edith Holländer in the 1920's.

"I can remember that as early as 1932, groups of storm troopers (Brownshirts) came marching by singing: 'When Jewish blood splatters off the knife.' That made it more than clear to everyone. I immediately discussed it with my wife: 'How can we leave here?', but eventually there is of course the question: How will you be able to support yourself if you go away and give up more or less everything?" (Otto Frank)

The year that Anne is born, 1929, is marked by a worldwide economic crisis. Germany is hit hard: countless numbers of businesses go bankrupt and millions of people lose their jobs. Also business at the bank owned by the Frank family is continually on the decline. By 1934 the bank will no longer exist. For Anne and Margot Frank the years in Frankfurt are peaceful, they hardly notice the crisis. Anne truly loves the stories her grandmother tells her and often plays with her sister and the children in the neighborhood. Not only Jews live in their neighborhood, but also Catholics and Protestants.

In this climate of crisis the *Nationalsozialistische Deutsche Arbeiterpartei* (*NSDAP* or Nazi party) can flourish. This small, extreme-nationalistic political party, under the leadership of Adolf Hitler, professes to have the solution to all problems. According to the Nazis, the stipulations of the Peace Treaty of Versailles should be rescinded and the Jews

7

8

Unemployed people waiting in line outside the Employment Office in Hannover, circa 1930.

are the ones responsible for the lost war and for the economic and political malaise.

The *NSDAP* attracts more and more followers and during the parliamentary elections of July 1932 it becomes the largest party with 37.3 percent of the vote. The political middle collapses; polarization increases. Otto and Edith Frank are seriously concerned about their future in Germany and that of their children.

Hilde Stab in 1931

"Margot was very impressed."

Hilde Stab, one of Margot's childhood friends, is Catholic. While indoors they often play "church". Then Hilde builds an "altar" in her room and in the role of priest sets forth the house rules. Margot is given the part of altar girl. Hilde invites Margot to her Communion party and gives her a photo of herself as a remembrance. On the back she writes: "For dearest Margot as a remembrance of Hilde's loveliest day." After the war, Hilde describes this day and their friendship: "Margot Frank lived on the same story in the apartment house next to ours and we were good friends. We played together often and got along very well. Anne was still too little then, she was two. I can still clearly remember my Communion party. That was an important day for me. I recall that Margot was very impressed." Later, Hilde does not join the *Bund Deutscher Mädchen*, a National-Socialist youth group for girls. Her classmates, whom for the most part become members, give her the cold shoulder.

9

10

NSDAP (Nazi party) in Nuremberg, 1927.

7 Margot and Anne Frank with some of the neighborhood children, 1930. In the photo (from left to right): Bernd (Buddy) Elias (their cousin), Maitly Könitzer, Gertrud Naumann, Anne, Marianne Stab, Werner Beck, Margot, Hilde Stab, Ingrid Naumann, and Butzy Könitzer.
8 Margot Frank, 1929.
9 Margot, Anne and Otto Frank, 1930.
→ Anne and Edith, 1931.

Gertrud Naumann
in 1933

"I knew and loved the Frank family, and have never forgotten them."
Gertrud Naumann is a neighbor of the Frank family. She often comes over to baby-sit for Anne and Margot, or to play with them. She is very sad about the Frank family's decision to leave. In retrospect, she says about this: "I would have loved to hold Anne in my arms one more time once she was in Holland. When she was little I changed her diapers, fed her, and played with her. I was attached to her and Margot, to the entire family and all their friends and acquaintances. The Frank family didn't actually want to go to the Netherlands. But what could they do? I knew and loved the Frank family and have never forgotten them." Countless letters are exchanged between Frankfurt and Amsterdam until the outbreak of World War Two makes this impossible. Otto Frank and Gertrud Naumann see each other for the last time in 1937 when Otto has to be in Germany on business. They will meet again, only after the war has ended.

"On January 30th (1933) we were unexpectedly invited over by acquaintances. We were sitting around the table listening to the radio. Then came the news that Hitler had become Chancellor. This was followed by a report about the Brownshirt's torch lit procession in Berlin and we could hear the screaming and cheering. Hitler ended his speech with the words: 'Just give me four years.' Our host then said enthusiastically: 'Let's see what that man can do!' I was speechless, my wife stunned." (Otto Frank)

Hitler becomes Chancellor of Germany on January 30, 1933. On March 5, 1933 there are elections for the *Reichstag* (Parliament) and a week later for the local city councils. The National Socialists win both

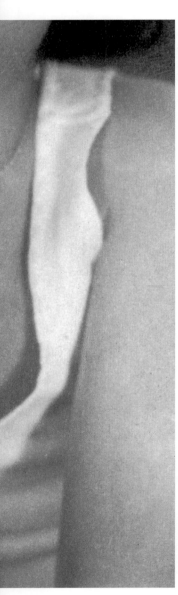

11

12

13

← Anne and Margot in Aachen, summer 1933.
12 A snapshot of Anne, Edith and Margot Frank made in an automatic photo booth in the Tietz department store, March 10, 1933.
13 Edith, with Anne and Margot on Hauptwache, a square in Frankfurt, March 10, 1933.
14 Margot Frank's bus pass, valid until Easter 1933.

An enthusiastic crowd welcomes Hitler to Berlin on the night of January 30, 1933.

elections. Frankfurt am Main is completely decked out in swastika flags. Two days earlier, Otto takes a photograph of Edith, Anne and Margot on Hauptwache, a well-known square in Frankfurt. At that moment the decision to emigrate has probably already been made, because in March the Frank family moves in with Otto's mother to economize on their living costs.

The new leaders quickly make their intentions known. Political opponents are persecuted and a witch hunt is launched against the Jews in Germany. When the foreign media report about the situation, the Nazis use this to their advantage by declaring a boycott of Jewish doctors, lawyers, shops and department stores on April 1, 1933.

A few days later the National-Socialist government

passes a law making it possible to fire both Jewish civil servants and those with oppositional views. Yet another law limits the percentage of Jewish students in schools and universities. After Easter 1933, some teachers seat their Jewish pupils apart. It is only at that very moment that many students realize that they, according to the Nazis, are "Jewish". Some of them have to switch schools and go to Jewish schools.

Elections for the Frankfurt city council are held on March 12, 1933. The *NDSAP* also wins here. A day later a swastika flag is hoisted in front of city hall.

"*Because we're full-blooded Jews, my father emigrated to Holland in 1933. He became the Managing Director of the Dutch Opekta Company, which manufactures products used in making jam. In September my mother went to Holland as well, while Margot and I were sent to Aachen. Margot went to Holland in December and I followed in February, when I was plunked down on the table as a birthday present for Margot.*" (Anne Frank)

In the summer of 1933, Otto and Edith Frank decide to leave Germany. Thanks to his brother-in-law Erich Elias, Otto has the opportunity to set up a franchise for selling pectin. Pectin is a jelling agent used in preparing jam. Otto travels to Amsterdam first. Edith, Anne and Margot go to grandmother Holländer in Aachen. Edith commutes back and forth to Amsterdam to assist Otto in finding a suitable residence for the family. He begins building up his business. M ep Santrouschitz and Victor Kugler become trusted employees, later Jo(hannes) Kleiman and Bep Voskuijl join them. In addition, several people work for Otto's company in the warehouse and in sales.

Once having taken power in January 1933, the National Socialists pursue an increasingly violent campaign against Jews and political opponents. Particularly Communists and Social Democrats are persecuted and imprisoned in concentration camps. Also certain types of art, literature, and music are banned. Books are burnt in public. Writers, artists, and scientists, many of them Jewish, flee abroad.

15

16

15 Otto Frank and Miep Santrouschitz in the office, 1933.
16 Otto Frank's entry card for a trade show in Rotterdam, September 1933.
17 Anne standing in front of her father's business on Singel Canal, circa 1934. The company will move to the building at 263 Prinsengracht at the end of November 1940.

In Germany, political opponents of the National Socialists are arrested, imprisoned, and in many cases tortured and murdered.

By the summer of 1933, the *NSDAP* is the only political party allowed in Germany.

In 1933, other assorted members of Anne Frank's family also leave Germany. Grandmother Frank-Stern moves to Basel (Switzerland), where Anne's aunt Helene and uncle Erich Elias have lived for three years. Herbert Frank has already left Germany in 1932. He lives in Paris. Uncle Robert and his wife leave for England in 1933. They begin an art dealership in London. Grandmother Holländer and both her sons Julius and Walter, Anne's uncles, still do not leave Germany. Once they are living in the Netherlands, Anne and Margot go on overnight visits to their grand-mothers in Aachen and Basel on several occasions.

Victor Kugler
in 1941

"Anne and Margot thought I was okay!"

Victor Kugler originally comes from Hohenelbe in Austria. He serves with the Austrian Navy during World War One. In 1920, he emigrates to the Netherlands and he goes to work for a company that sells pectin. When his boss withdraws from the business in 1933, Otto Frank becomes his new employer. Afterwards Victor Kugler adopts the Dutch nationality. Years later he can still remember in detail first meeting Margot and Anne Frank: "I saw Anne for the first time in March 1934. Mrs. Frank came to visit her husband and for the first time she brought along her daughters. The girls thought I was okay because we were quickly engaged in conversation. At that age there was a noticeable difference between the two girls. Margot, the oldest, was calmly looking around. In contrast, Anne was enthusiastic and investigated everything that interested her. Later on, Mrs. Frank brought her along more often. That child was really happy to see her father and her father was just as happy to see his youngest daughter. Anne was always a welcome distraction with her lively chattering."

rs van de Dameskroniek

9 Sept. tot en met Zondag 8 Oct. 1933

Hal B „Nenijto" - Rotterdam

ANTENKAART

rloopend geldig)

nk

pekta".

t persoonlijk.   DE DIRECTIE.

In May 1933, in Germany's large cities, books written by writers whom the Nazis consider to be "un-German" are burnt.

"The Van Pelses and the Franks were good friends."

Hermann van Pels and his wife Auguste and their son Peter (b. 1926) are from Osnabrück, a city close to the Dutch border. They emigrate from Germany in 1937. Hermann van Pels is Dutch by birth and his wife receives the Dutch nationality through marriage. The Van Pels family lives in the same block of apartments as the Frank family. The gardens behind the buildings border on each other. The families strike up a friendship rather quickly. The decision to merge their companies is made later on. Hermann van Pels becomes Otto's business partner in 1938. "The Van Pelses and the Franks were good friends, the men as well as the women," relates Max van Creveld, who boarded with the Van Pels family in 1940 and 1941. "I had my own room and every evening we ate together. Mr. van Pels was a very charming person just like Mrs. van Pels. Peter was a fine boy. I can't recall anymore which school he went to, but I can remember that he was taking a course in upholstering then."

The further isolation of Jews from non-Jews continues in Germany. Signboards in many cities and towns indicate that Jews are not welcome.

"In the Netherlands, after those experiences in Germany, it was as if our life was restored to us. Our children went to school and at least in the beginning our lives proceeded normally. In those days it was possible for us to start over and to feel free." (Otto Frank)

The Frank family lives on Merwedeplein in a newly built neighborhood of Amsterdam. More and more Jewish refugees fleeing Germany come to live in the city. Anne and Margot go to school and learn Dutch very quickly. They have both Dutch and German friends. The Frank family keeps abreast of what is happening in Germany by corresponding with friends there. Edith misses living in Frankfurt. She tries to

adjust and takes Dutch lessons, but gives up after only two attempts.

Prosperity in Germany increases. There is great enthusiasm for Hitler and his party. Measures enacted against fellow Jewish citizens by the *NSDAP* meet with little or no resistance. In 1935, for instance, the "Nuremberg Race Laws" are declared. Only Germans with so-called "German-blood" are full-fledged citizens. All the rest are second-class citizens. There are more and more measures enacted to limit contact between Jews and non-Jews or to make it a criminal offense. These regulations are effective even though some people do try to offer resistance. The Jews in Germany are driven further and further into isolation.

Otto and Edith Frank meet Hermann and Auguste van Pels and their son Peter: the future co-inhabitants in hiding. The Van Pels family has fled Osnabrück in 1937. Hermann van Pels becomes Otto Frank's business partner in 1938. His special knowledge of spices used for preparing meats and sausage makes Otto Frank's company less seasonally dependent.

20

21

There is massive enthusiasm in Germany about the country's economic recovery and recaptured self-esteem. Many see the strict regulations against political opponents and Jews as a necessary evil.

18 Anne, in Mr. Gelder's second grade class at the Montessori School, 1936.
19 Margot Frank, 1934.
20 Peter van Pels (middle) and his friends in Osnabrück (Germany), circa 1936.
→ Anne in the sandbox with friends, July 1937. From left to right: Hannah Goslar, Anne, Dolly Citroen, Hannah Toby, Barbara and Susanne Ledermann.

"Our lives were not without anxiety, since our relatives in Germany were suffering under Hitler's anti-Jewish laws. After the pogroms in 1938, my two uncles – brothers of my mother – fled and found safe refuge in North America." (Anne Frank)

During the night of November 9, 1938, 236 people in Germany are murdered and 177 synagogues, 7,500 stores, and countless number of homes are destroyed by the Nazis. Based on prepared lists approximately 30,000 Jewish men are arrested and deported to concentration camps. Among them are Anne's uncles, Julius and Walter Holländer. Julius is released right away because he is a war veteran. Walter is deported to the Sachsenhausen concentration camp. He is impris-

oned for longer and is only released when he declares that he will leave Germany immediately. The magnitude of the danger is now more than apparent to them. They decide to flee Germany.

Walter ends up in a refugee camp in Amsterdam. It takes more than a year, until December 1939, before he can travel by ship to the United States. His brother has already made the boat trip to New York in April 1939. With much difficulty they succeed in building up a livelihood outside of Boston. More and more countries close their borders to refugees. Sometimes an exception is still made for children. Between 1933 and 1939 half of all the Jews in Germany leave the country.

Jewish refugees seem to be safe in Amsterdam.

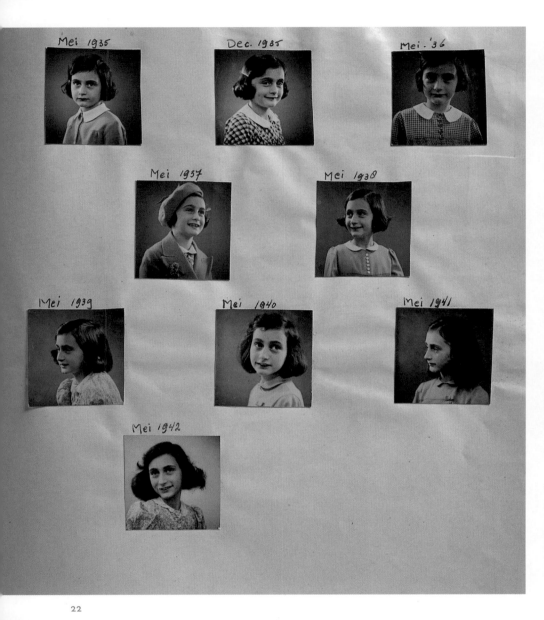

22

23

22 Anne Frank.
23 Margot Frank.
24 Fritz Pfeffer and his Catholic girlfriend
    Charlotte Kaletta.

On November 7, 1938, Herschel Grynzspan, a seventeen-year-old Polish Jewish youngster, guns down an official who works at the German Embassy in Paris. The boy is desperate because his parents have been deported from Germany. The Nazis use this as a pretext for organizing a pogrom against Germany's Jews, which takes place on November 9, 1938 and is later called *Kristallnacht* or "Crystal Night".

Sometimes on Saturday afternoons the Frank family holds open house with coffee and cake. There are usually numerous guests, mainly German Jews. Counted among them are: Hermann and Auguste van Pels, as well as Fritz Pfeffer and Charlotte Kaletta. Also Miep Santrouschitz and her fiancé Jan Gies are often invited.

Charlotte Kaletta around 1940

"My husband was Jewish; I'm Catholic."

Fritz Pfeffer is a Jewish dentist from Berlin. He is divorced and has a son Werner who lives with him. His Catholic girlfriend Charlotte Kaletta is also divorced and has a son. According to the Nuremberg Race Laws these two people are not allowed to marry. Concerning their different faiths, Charlotte says after the war: "We talked about this when it was of use and didn't mention it when that was handier." In December 1938, Fritz Pfeffer and Charlotte Kaletta emigrate to the Netherlands. Werner, who is eleven at that time, is sent to live with an uncle in England. In the Netherlands, most people do not want to believe Charlotte and Fritz when they describe the situation in Germany: "We left Berlin after a terrible night in November 1938 and emigrated to the Netherlands. Many Dutch people did not believe what we were telling them about the events in Germany, even many Jews could not believe it." Fritz Pfeffer and Charlotte Kaletta attempt to marry first in the Netherlands and then in Belgium, but without success. Both of these countries respect the racist German legislation of 1935.

Dec. 1936

Mei 1939

Following *Kristallnacht* thousands of Jews flee Germany. Other countries are quickly inclined to close down their borders to refugees. Ultimately, it is often only children that are still accepted. These girls are part of a group of five hundred children from Vienna who arrive in Harwich (Great Britain) on December 12th.

Hannah Goslar
in 1939

Friends Since Nursery School

While still in nursery school, Anne Frank meets Hannah Goslar, who later becomes one of her best friends. Just like Anne, Hannah arrives in 1933 with her parents from Germany. The Goslar family also lives on Merwedeplein. The families are practically neighbors. Hannah Goslar still remembers her first day of nursery school quite clearly: "I walked in, Anne stood opposite the door jingling some bells. She turned around, I flew into her arms and my mother could go home without worrying." Afterwards the girls went to elementary school together. Sometimes Anne and Hannah played in Otto Frank's office in the building on the Prinsengracht, the future hiding place. Hannah says about this after the war: "We often went with her father on Sundays to the office of Mr. Frank, and there we played. Every room in the office had a telephone, which gave us the opportunity to play our favorite game – telephoning from room to room. That was quite an experience." In 1941, when Jewish children are forced to attend Jewish schools, Anne and Hannah go to the Jewish Lyceum (high school) together.

25

26

25 Grandmother Holländer arrives in the Netherlands in March 1939.

26 The birthday girl Anne and her girlfriends on June 12, 1939. From left to right: Lucie van Dijk, Anne Frank, Susanne Ledermann, Hannah Goslar, Juultje Ketellapper, Kitty Egyedi, Mary Bos, Ietje Swillens, and Martha van den Bergh.

27 The Frank family on Merwedeplein, circa 1940.

German soldiers humiliate, mishandle and in some cases even murder Polish Jews. Offenses are also committed against the non-Jewish populace.

"After May 1940 good times rapidly fled: first the war,
then the capitulation, followed by the German invasion
which is when the suffering of us Jews really began."
(Anne Frank)

In March 1939, Grandmother Holländer flees to the
Netherlands and moves in with the Frank family.
She is forced to leave almost all her possessions behind.
Anne and Margot are busy going to school, play a
lot with their friends, and are hardly aware of the great
threat. On June 12 1939, Anne Frank celebrates her
tenth birthday. She invites along eight of her friends.
Half of them, just like her, have recently arrived from
Germany. It is to be her last birthday not clouded
by wartime.

On August 23, 1939, Germany signs a nonaggression
pact with the Soviet Union. On September 1, 1939, the
German army invades Poland. The army empties large
territories in order to settle German colonists there.
The Jewish inhabitants are obliged to move to ghettos,
fenced off neighborhoods in cities. Prominent Poles,
many of them Jewish, are murdered. At that moment
there are more than three million Jews living in Poland.
Apart from that, the other half of Poland is occupied
by the Russian Army.

In Western Europe there is little awareness of
the atrocities that are being committed in Poland.
Like many of the Dutch, Otto and Edith Frank assume
the Netherlands will remain neutral, as it had been
during World War One. Yet, in May 1940 the war

begins in the West. The German Army occupies the
Netherlands, Belgium, and France. The Nazis see the
non-Jewish inhabitants of these countries, in contrast to
the Poles, as "kindred people" and they do not commit
similar atrocities. However, all inhabitants are required
to fill-in a so-called Aryan declaration. They have to
state if they have any Jewish grandparents and if so, how
many? In this manner all of the 140,000 Jews living in
the Netherlands are registered.

The German Army entering Amsterdam on May 16,
1940. Seen in the background is the tower of the
"Westerkerk", the church nearby the Secret Annex.

"Anti-Jewish decrees followed each other in quick succession and our freedom was strictly limited: Jews must wear a yellow star; Jews must hand in their bicycles; Jews are banned from streetcars; Jews cannot ride in cars, even their own; Jews may only do their shopping between 3:00 p.m. and 5:00 p.m.; Jews may only go to barbershops and beauty parlors owned by Jews; Jew have to stay indoors from 8:00 p.m. to 6:00 a.m.; Jews may not go to theaters, movies, or frequent any other forms of entertainment; Jews may not use swimming pools, tennis courts, hockey fields or any other sport facilities; Jews are not allowed to go rowing; Jews may not take part in any public sporting events; Jews are not allowed to sit in their gardens or those of their friends after 8:00 p.m.; Jews are not allowed to visit Christians at home; Jews must attend Jewish schools, etc." (Anne Frank)

In all of the occupied countries, one of the first steps taken by the Germans in power is the registration of the Jews. Isolation is the next step. Much like earlier on in Germany, continuing steps are taken against the Jews to segregate them from the non-Jewish populace. In September 1941, Anne and Margot begin attending a special Jewish high school, the Jewish Lyceum. Throughout the city hang signs saying: "No Jews Allowed". Jews may also no longer have their own businesses. Otto Frank therefore appoints Jo Kleiman director of Opekta, but he remains active behind the scenes. Also the spice concern Pectacon changes ownership and is called Gies & Co., after Miep's husband Jan Gies. In the summer of 1941, Otto Frank begins furnishing a hiding place in the empty annex behind his company at 263 Prinsengracht.

28

29

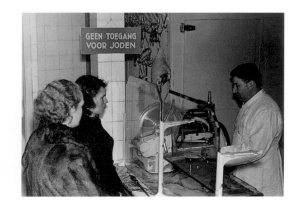

Just like earlier in Germany, a series of anti-Jewish measures is rapidly declared also in the occupied countries. (Signboard: "No Admittance to Jews")

Miep Gies in 1941

"I said: of course."

In the summer of 1941, Otto Frank and Jo Kleiman begin covertly bringing food and other necessities to the Secret Annex. Furniture and carpets are delivered by truck. Besides Edith Frank and Hermann and Auguste van Pels, only Jo Kleiman is aware of the plans to go into hiding. Miep Gies says after the war: "One morning Otto Frank called me over and informed me about the plans to go into hiding: 'Miep, my wife, and I are planning to go into hiding with Anne and Margot. We're going to do this with Van Pels and his wife and son.' Otto asked me if I had any objections to this." Miep recalls about that moment: "I said that I didn't have any objections. Otto took a deep breath and asked me: 'Miep, would you be prepared to assume the responsibility for taking care of us for as long as we're in hiding?' Of course, I said. 'Miep, there are harsh punishments for helping Jews: imprisonment, even...' I interrupted him. I said: of course. And I meant it. 'Good. Only Kleiman knows about this. Even Anne and Margot don't know yet. I'll ask the others one by one.'"

30

31

Beginning on May 3, 1942, all Jews in the Netherlands above the age of five must wear a yellow star, with the word *Jood* or 'Jew'.

28 Anne and her friend Hannah on Merwedeplein, 1939.

29 Anne in her last year at the Montessori School. After the summer vacation of 1941, Jewish children must go to separate schools.

30 Miep Santrouschitz marries Jan Gies on July 16, 1942. Anne and Otto are among the wedding guests. Edith stays at home: Margot and Grandma are sick.

→ Otto and Anne walking among the other wedding guests. July 16, 1941.

Jacqueline Sanders-
van Maarsen
in 1999

"She would never know how important the diary would become."
In celebration of her thirteenth birthday Anne throws a party for all her friends.
In her diary she writes: *"We saw a film 'The Lighthouse Keeper' with Rin Tin Tin,
which my school friends thoroughly enjoyed."* In addition Otto Frank shows a promo-
tional film about his company. Anne writes further: *"We had a lot of fun and it was
truly festive. There were lots of boys and girls."* One of these girls and one of Anne's
best friends is Jacqueline van Maarsen. After the war she reminisces: "Anne, to me,
will always be that girlfriend from long ago. I remember her thirteenth birthday.
Her eyes were sparkling as she watched her friends filing in and she was filled with
anticipation as she opened the packages. She loved being the center of attention and
was still revelling in it, once everyone had left and we were tidying up her presents
together. I can still remember this so well, because I didn't see her diary lying among
the other gifts anymore, which surprised me because it was her most important gift.
How important it would become, that she would never know."

*"In the summer of 1941 Grandma (Holländer) got very
sick. She had to have an operation and nothing much
was done about my birthday. Also in the summer of
1940 not much of anything happened, because the war
had just begun in Holland. Grandma died in January
1942. Nobody knows how often I think of her and still
love her. So this birthday in 1942 was celebrated to
make up for all the others, and Grandma's candle was
lit along with the rest."* (Anne Frank)

On June 12, 1942, Anne turns thirteen years old. On this
birthday she also receives gifts from Peter van Pels
and Charlotte Kaletta. Her parents give her a diary for
her thirteenth birthday. In that diary she writes about
everything she experiences, feels, and thinks. For a few

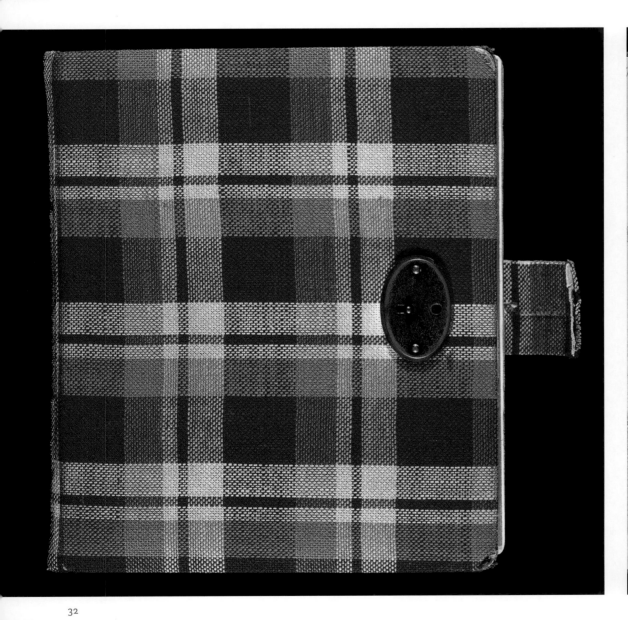

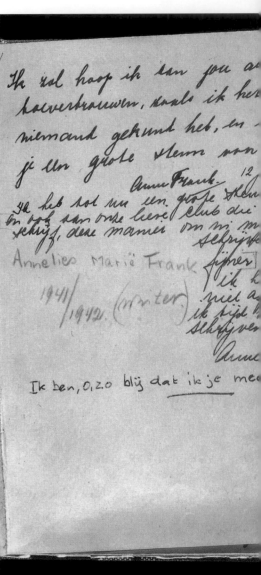

32 On her thirteenth birthday Anne receives a diary
    as a gift.
33 *"I hope I will be able to confide everything to you,
    as I have never been able to confide in anyone, and
    I hope you will be a great comfort to me."*
34 Anne Frank, May 1942.
35 Anne and Margot Frank, circa 1942.

Deportation of the Jewish residents of Hanau
(Germany), May 30, 1942.

weeks, her diary entries revolve around school, classmates and friends; after that her life changes dramatically.

By the end of 1941, the registration and segregation of the Jews in Germany and in most of the occupied territories is completed. During the secretive "Wannsee Conference" in Berlin on January 20, 1942, top Nazi officials work out the "final solution to the Jewish question". Probably the decision to murder all eleven million European Jews is taken earlier, in the summer of 1941. The plans for deportation and extermination are now put into effect. In most of the occupied countries and in Germany, Jews receive a call-up notice to report for work camps. In actuality,

from the beginning of October 1941, Jews are systematically deported to concentration and extermination camps, most of which are built in occupied Poland. In these camps many people are murdered immediately or die after a short while from malnutrition, exhaustion, or diseases.

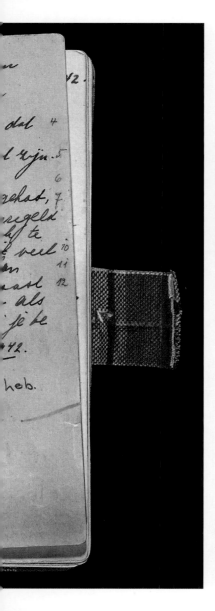

34

35

After the invasion of the Soviet Union in June 1941, special German army units execute a million Jews, as well as hundreds of thousands of other inhabitants and prisoners of war.

"Sunday morning Hello and I lay on our balcony in the sun. He was supposed to return Sunday afternoon, but instead at around 3 o'clock a police officer came to see mother and he shouted from downstairs in the doorway: 'Miss Margot Frank!'. Mother went downstairs and she got a card from the officer, written on it was that Margot Frank had to report to the SS. Mother was totally upset and went directly to Mr. van Pels, he came to see us immediately."
(Anne Frank)

On July 5, 1942, thousands of Jews in the Netherlands, principally young Jewish refugees from Germany, receive a call-up notice to report for the *"werk-verruiming"* ('work force project'). Among them are some youngsters who, just like the sixteen-year-old Margot Frank, receive a call-up on that Sunday afternoon. They will have to go without their parents. Late that afternoon Anne's friend Hello comes by again, but he is not allowed inside. Anne also receives a telephone call from her friend Jacqueline that same afternoon. They chat a while but Anne is not supposed to tell her anything.

Margot and Anne are sent out of the room because Hermann van Pels wants to discuss the situation with Edith alone. Anne and Margot suspect then that they are going to go into hiding and they already begin to gather their things for packing. In her school satchel, Anne packs her diary, hair curlers, handkerchiefs, schoolbooks, a comb, and some old letters. At five o'clock, Otto Frank returns home. He was visiting an acquaintance at the Jewish Hospital. Otto and Edith decide to go directly into hiding the next day. They ring Kleiman and ask him if he will come over that evening so they can discuss everything. Van Pels then leaves to go pick up Miep Gies. Miep brings clothes along to take to the hiding place and promises to come back that night. At 11 o'clock Miep and her husband Jan return to take more things to the hiding place.

The call-up notice lists precisely what Jews may bring along with them. The impression is given that they are going to a work camp.

Hello Silberberg
in 1942

"The door remained shut."

Anne meets Helmuth (Hello) Silberberg on June 23, 1942. Following *Kristallnacht*, Hello's parents put him on a train to Amsterdam, where he will live with his grandparents. More than fifty-years later Hello describes first meeting Anne Frank: "I immediately thought she was very special, even though she was four years younger. As far as age goes I should have actually liked Margot. Anne was still a little girl, but I was fascinated by her, the way she could practically disappear into the large armchairs in her living room. She imitated everyone. I always had to laugh, because she could pull her arm in and out of the socket." From that day on Anne and Hello bike to school together. Sometimes in the evenings they take a stroll. Hello also still remembers that he returned on that Sunday afternoon and was not allowed to see Anne: "I was disappointed and wondered what had happened. The following day I rang the bell a few different times, but the door remained shut. I wasn't really worried, I had become accustomed to the fact that people suddenly disappeared without a trace."

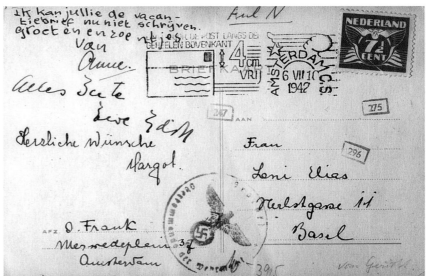

Many of those who receive a call-up notice simply do not report. Consequently, the occupying force attempts to pick up Jews using razzias: a neighborhood is sealed off and the houses are searched door to door.

36 Anne Frank on the "balcony" (roof) of the house on Merwedeplein, circa 1940.

37 Already in the summer of 1941, Otto Frank and the future helpers begin to furnish the hiding place on the Prinsengracht.

38 The last greetings sent to the family in Basel. Also during the hiding period the Frank family actually still finds ways to get information about the ups and downs of the family in Basel.

Monday, July 6, 1942.

"So there we were walking though the pouring rain, Father, Mother and I, each of us with a school satchel and a shopping bag filled to the brim with the most varied assortment of items. The people on their way to work at that early hour gave us sympathetic looks; you could tell by their faces that they were sorry they couldn't offer us some kind of transportation; the conspicuous yellow star spoke for itself." (Anne Frank)

On Monday July 6th, Anne is awakened at five-thirty in the morning by her mother. It is less warm than Sunday, it rains throughout the day. In order to take as much as possible with them the family dresses in thick layers of clothing. Anne puts on two undershirts, three pairs of underpants, over that a skirt, a jacket, a raincoat, two pairs of stockings, heavy shoes, a cap, a scarf, and even more. Miep Gies comes along and takes Margot, on the bicycle, to the hiding place.

At seven-thirty, the rest of the family leaves the house on Merwedeplein and goes on foot to the Secret Annex located behind Otto Frank's company on the Prinsengracht. The house is left in such a state that it appears as if they have all fled in haste. One week later the Van Pels family – Hermann, Auguste and their son Peter – also comes to hide in the Secret Annex. On November 16, 1942, yet an eighth person joins all of them in hiding, Fritz Pfeffer. These eight people are taken care of by Otto Frank's most trusted employees:

39 Otto Frank's company on the Prinsengracht.
40 The hiding place, the annex of Otto Frank's company.

Miep Gies, Jo Kleiman, Victor Kugler and Bep Voskuijl.
The people in hiding will spend more than two years
in the Secret Annex.

*"Though it's damp and lopsided, the Secret Annex is
ideal as a hide-out. In all of Amsterdam, perhaps even
in all of Holland, nobody could have ever furnished
a place for hiding people that's so comfortable."*
(Anne Frank)

The People Who Go into Hiding

The Helpers

Otto Frank

Hermann van Pels

Miep Gies-Santrouschitz

Edith Frank-Holländer

Auguste van Pels-Röttgen

Jo Kleiman

Margot Frank

Peter van Pels

Victor Kugler

Anne Frank

Fritz Pfeffer

Bep Voskuijl

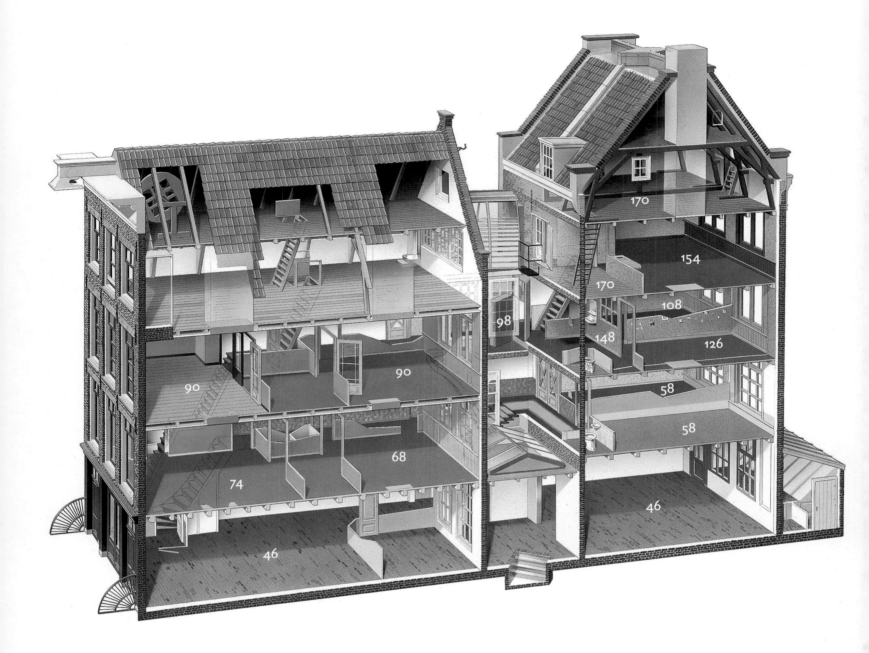

The Front Part of the House
and the Annex

Going into Hiding

"The large warehouse on the ground floor is used as a workroom and storeroom and is divided into several different sections, such as the stockroom and the milling room where cinnamon, cloves and a pepper substitute are ground."

July 9, 1942

The Warehouse

The warehouse on the ground floor is run by several warehousemen supervised by the warehouse manager Johan Voskuijl, the father of the helper Bep Voskuijl, who herself works in the office. These workers grind the spices for Gies & Co. and handle the distribution of Opekta goods. The office (staff) and warehouse (men) basically function independent of each other. Members of the office staff

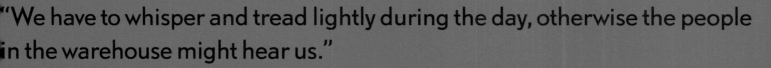

"We have to whisper and tread lightly during the day, otherwise the people in the warehouse might hear us."

July 11, 1942

seldom go to the warehouse. Apart from Johan Voskuijl, the warehouse workers do not know anything about the hiding place. They are therefore a constant source of anxiety for those in hiding, just like the neighbors. When Johan Voskuijl becomes very ill, Willem van Maaren takes his place. All the inhabitants of the Secret Annex distrust Van Maaren.

1 Economic activity on the Prinsengracht in the 1930's. Otto Frank moves his company to 263 Prinsengracht in December 1940. Many storehouses and small businesses – such as coffee and tea trading companies, spice trading companies and small manufacturers – can be found on this part of the Prinsengracht. The transportation of goods is carried out by boat and with bicycle carts.

"We're very afraid that the neighbors might hear or see us. Right next door there's a branch of the Keg Company from Zaandam, to the left there's a furniture workshop. The people who work there aren't on the premises after hours, but any sound we make could still travel through the walls. Therefore we've also forbidden Margot to cough at night, although she has a terrible cold, and we're giving her large doses of codeine." (July 11, 1942)

2 The rear of the warehouse, where ground spices are weighed and packaged. Hermann van Pels is responsible for this part of the business. During the war there is a great demand for substitute spices. The trade in genuine spices, for the most part commodities originating from the then Netherlands East Indies, has come to a virtual standstill because of the war.

3 The pectin used in making jam and jelly is packaged in small packets and in bottles. Opekta also supplies membranes used for making an airtight seal when preserving pots of jam. The firm distributes their products to drugstores and grocery stores and provides advice to housewives.

4 Sometimes Anne is enthusiastic about her father's business: *"There isn't such a swell company like ours anywhere in the world"*. (September 25, 1942)

She even hangs an Opekta poster in her own room.
At other times she thinks her father's business is boring.

The Pectacon firm, which trades in spice and herb
mixtures, is registered for the duration of the war and
afterwards as Gies & Co., in the name of the non-Jewish
helpers. Worked into the logo of the company is its
location: by the tower of the Westerkerk, the church
nearby. Special brand names are created for the various
spice mixtures such as *EFWEKA* for the sausage spices.

*"Dear Kitty, We've got something new to do, namely
filling packets with gravy (in powder form). This gravy
is made by Gies & Company. Mr. Kugler can't find
any fillers, and besides, it's also a lot cheaper if we
do the job. It's the kind of work they do in prison, it's
exceptionally boring and makes you dizzy and giddy."*
(January 13, 1943)

2

1 The spice grinding room of Gies & Co located in the middle section of the warehouse. Also mentioned in Anne's diary – besides cinnamon, cloves, and substitute-pepper – are the odors of real pepper and thyme.

"We can't breathe or we're constantly sneezing and coughing, because so much pepper is ground through the machines. Everyone who comes upstairs greets us with 'ah-choo'. Madam (Mrs. van Pels) swears she won't go downstairs, she'll get sick if she smells any more pepper. I don't think Father has a very nice business, nothing but pectin and pepper. As long as you're in the food business, why not make candy?" (March 4, 1943)

2 An invoice dated October 20, 1942, for nutmeg butter purchased for Gies & Co. by the commodity-broker.

3 The following spices and herbs are sold by Gies & Co: nutmeg, white and black pepper, allspice, cinnamon, Cassia Lignea, Moroccan coriander, mace, boric acid flakes, cloves, ground red pepper, coriander seed, turmeric root, powdered ginger root, and nutmeg butter.

4 Danger of discovery presents itself not only from the street side, but also from the gardens in the back. During the day the workers in the warehouse must not hear the people in hiding. The windows of the Secret Annex are concealed from the view of the warehouse-men because of an extension built onto the rear of their work space. Of course the neighbors must also not notice anything suspicious. Making any noise at night is therefore just as dangerous. The longer the war lasts, the more times the building is burglarized. These break-ins are a continual threat to those in hiding.

"Once again, we've had more than enough excitement because there's been a break-in. What's happened now? This thief must have had a copy of the key because the door was not forced. It's a mystery. Who here could have our key? And why didn't the thief go to the warehouse? If the thief is one of the warehousemen he now knows that someone's in the building at night." (March 1, 1944)

5 Hans Wijnberg is one of the non-Jewish children who lives nearby on the Prinsengracht. He drops by the warehouse frequently and runs around in the neighborhood gardens out back. During the war it becomes ever more difficult to get food. Hans and his sister Els want to help out their mother, so they go rummaging in the warehouse of Opekta and Gies & Company.

Hans Wijnberg
in 1998

Els Schönbeck-
Wijnberg in 1998

Years later, Hans and Els Wijnberg describe their "break-in": "We lived here in the neighborhood. I (Hans) was ten or so and walked in and out of the warehouses and workshops. So then I also saw the warehouse at number 263. I can recall the smell of pepper, cloves, and cinnamon sticks. The "break-in" was more like sneaking in than breaking-in, because it was easy, without forcing anything. I knew that there must be spices stored somewhere in the warehouse and at a certain moment, in the evening or in the weekend, I wanted to go get some of them. I went through the garden, with my sister Els. She crept through a small window and opened the door. We had already taken a few nutmeg apples and then I suddenly heard the toilet being flushed. The pipe ran down the back just like in our house. I therefore understood immediately that there were people in the building and thought: Let's get out of here! We didn't say anything about this. We were used to keeping our mouths shut because periodically we also had somebody in hiding at our house. We shouldn't have been in that warehouse in the first place."

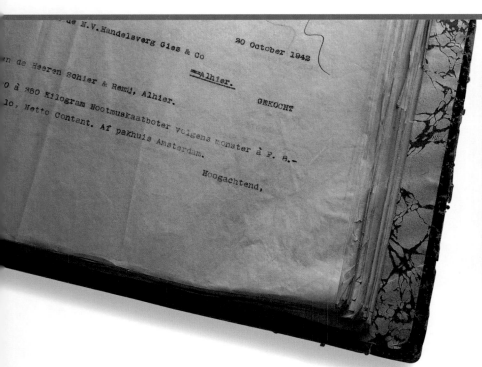

5

3

4

1   The layout of the building on the Prinsengracht is so complicated that a new worker cannot readily discover the hiding place, especially since the warehouse-men actually have no reason to go upstairs. The only warehouse employee advised of the situation is Johan Voskuijl, who falls ill in 1943 and is then no longer able to work. On June 15th of that year Anne writes: *"It's a disaster for us now that the good Mr. Voskuijl can no longer tell us about what's being done and said in the warehouse. He was our greatest source of help and support when it came to safety measures. We miss him very much."* The warehouse personnel change repeatedly during the hiding period.

"We're getting a new warehouse worker, since the present one is being sent to Germany. That's a shame for him but for us it's actually good because a new one won't be familiar with the building. We're still afraid of the men who work in the warehouse. Our green grocer knows that we're in hiding and that's why he always comes along during the lunch break when the warehouse employees are out." (March 4, 1943)

2   The front section of the warehouse with a bicycle cart used for deliveries of packaged spices and Opekta-articles. Gasoline becomes increasingly scarce during the war and people transport things using "manpower" or "horsepower".

3   The entry of the warehouse in the early 1950's with one of the warehousemen (unknown). During the war years, the large warehouse doors are usually wide-open in the daytime. Consequently, the warehouse men are witness to peculiar goings-on. Take for instance Lammert Hartog, who starts working in the warehouse in the Spring of 1944. He notices that the baker delivers

1

3

a lot of bread and he discusses this with his wife Lena, who cleans the building. The new warehouse manager Van Maaren is also suspicious. He suspects that there are people in the building at night.

"Probably Van Maaren also has suspicions about us; he puts books and bits of paper close to the edge of things in the warehouse so if anyone walks by they fall off. Together with Kleiman, who just came by, Kugler and the two gentlemen have been looking into the question of how to get rid of this guy. Downstairs they think it's too risky. Yet isn't it even riskier to leave things as they are?" (April 25, 1944)

Willem van Maaren
around 1965

In 1948, at the request of Jo Kleiman and Otto Frank, a judicial inquiry is conducted into the betrayal of those in hiding on the Prinsengracht. Willem van Maaren is one of the suspects. Van Maaren categorically denies any involvement in the betrayal. An excerpt from his March 31, 1948 testimony: "I came to work for Opekta as a warehouseman in the spring of 1943. My activities were exclusively confined to the warehouse on the ground floor of the building. However, during the year 1943-1944, I did begin to suspect that there was something unusual happening on the premises, although I didn't think about Jews in hiding. These suspicions arose because the baker, the milkman, and the green grocer were delivering rather large amounts of food provisions to the building." Van Maaren also stresses that other visitors came to the premises and that the neighbors presented a threat as well. The question of who committed the betrayal has never been answered. Nothing could be proven.

1 The people in hiding sometimes visit the warehouse in the evenings. On one occasion Hermann van Pels loses his wallet there. Peter always goes downstairs to control everything before the inhabitants of the Secret Annex go to sleep. At night the warehouse is the domain of cats and rats.

"Krauty is the warehouse and office cat and keeps the storeroom rat free. Her odd political name is also easy to explain. For a while Gies & Co. had two cats, one for the warehouse and one for the attic. Their paths crossed from time to time, which invariably resulted in large fights. The warehouse cat was always the aggressor, yet in the end the attic cat always came out on top, just like in politics. So the warehouse cat became the German or 'Krauty' and the attic cat became the Englishman, and was named 'Tommy'."
(March 12, 1943)

1

3

2

4

On one particular evening there is a blackout due to a short circuit. *"We did have new fuses available, but the fuses had to be screwed-in all the way in the back of the dark warehouse and that was no easy chore at night. Yet the men dared to do it and ten minutes later our festively lit candles could be put away."* (October 20, 1942)

Simply looking at the exterior of a canal house reveals little about its interior floor plan. Every canal house is different. The two doors left of the warehouse doors each open directly onto a staircase. The left-hand door is the entry to a long steep "leg-breaking" stairway that continues up to the third floor. The right-hand door opens onto a short staircase that leads to the office on the second floor. The office staff uses this staircase. People can enter the warehouse through the larger doors on the right. Therefore the office and the warehouse have completely separate entrances.

3 This door in the warehouse leads to a stairway going to the office floor. During the day sometimes staff from the office has to confer with personnel in the warehouse. Then this corridor is used.

"Also in the front part of the house there's another long, extremely steep, typically Dutch 'leg-breaking' staircase going down to a second street-level door." (July 9, 1942)

4 The long, steep "leg-breaking" staircase.

5 The stairway leading to the offices on the second floor. Unannounced visitors don't get any further than the door marked "Office".

5

"Go up four steps, you find yourself in the private office, the showpiece of the entire building. Elegant mahogany furniture, a linoleum floor covered with throw rugs, a radio, a fancy lamp, everything first class. Next door is a spacious kitchen with a hot-water heater and two gas burners, and beside that a bathroom."

July 9, 1942

The Private Office and the Kitchen

Once the personnel go home, those in hiding often come out of their hide-out.

Then they go off to the office or other company spaces, or to the private office –

Anne's name for the director's office. This office on the second floor, directly

under the hiding place, is occasionally used for business meetings. Besides this,

supplies are sometimes left there for the people in hiding. The kitchen is especially

"Last night the four of us went down to the private office and listened to England on the radio. I was so scared that someone could hear us that I literally begged Father to go back upstairs with me; Mother understood my fear and went with me."

July 11, 1942

mportant for laundry. In the evenings and weekends the people in hiding can bathe, work, and listen to the radio in the private office. Sometimes they wash up in the kitchen and now and then Anne bathes in the lavatory. Warm water is hauled from the kitchen. Occasionally, Anne and Peter take a look outside by peeking through the curtains.

1   Jo Kleiman and A.W. Kwakernaak in the private
office, 1954.

Anne writes that on two occasions Pomosin-Werke
sales representatives from Frankfurt come to discuss
new Opekta deliveries. She notes on April 1, 1943:
*"The gentlemen arrived from Frankfurt and Father was
already nervous about the outcome of the meeting.
'If only I could be there, if only I were downstairs,' he
exclaimed. 'Go lie on the ground with your ear to the
floor, they'll be brought to the private office and then
you can hear everything.' Father cheered up, and
yesterday morning at ten-thirty Margot with Pim
(Father) – two ears are better than one – took up their
posts on the floor."*

*"The meeting was not finished in the morning, but
by the afternoon father was in no condition to continue*

*the eavesdropping campaign. He was exhausted
from lying in such an unusual and uncomfortable
position. I took his place at two-thirty. Margot kept
me company. The discussion in part was so drawn
out and boring that I suddenly fell asleep on the
hard, cold linoleum floor. Margot didn't dare to
touch me for fear that they'd hear us downstairs,
and saying anything to me was out of the question.
I slept for a good half-hour, then woke with a start
and had forgotten everything of the important
meeting. Luckily Margot had paid more attention."*
(April 1, 1943)

→   The helpers can reach the hiding place by way of
this stairway which goes to the landing in front of the
bookcase. In the evenings the people in hiding can
sneak down to the private office or the kitchen by
using these stairs.

In the beginning, the people in hiding listen to the radio in the private office. Anne writes on September 1, 1942: "I listen to the radio every Saturday night, then there's a variety-show program from Germany, but each time it gets even duller, ever since the first evening when the program was called: 'In Love, Engaged, Married', but then of course in German." Later on there is a radio in the Secret Annex, in the room belonging to the Van Pels family. Every day those in hiding listen to the news broadcasts.

"Last Saturday the foreign gentlemen came to visit again. They stayed until six o'clock. We were all sitting upstairs and didn't dare to move. If there's nobody else on the premises or working in the neighborhood then in the private office you can hear every single step. I've got ants-in-my-pants again; sitting still as a mouse for so long isn't exactly easy." (April 27, 1943)

3 At least twice during the hiding period, business associates of Otto Frank – from Pomosin-Werke in Frankfurt am Main – come to Amsterdam. One of them talks about this after the war: "Otto Frank and I were business associates, also after he'd emigrated to the Netherlands. I met with him a few more times in Amsterdam, but one day he was suddenly gone. Otto's co-workers Victor Kugler and Jo Kleiman still worked in the office on the Prinsengracht and therefore I had to negotiate with them. During the meetings we talked about Otto Frank, who as a Jew wasn't allowed to manage his own business anymore. You can imagine how unpleasant I found these meetings. I tried as best I could to still do something for his company. After the war I read Anne's diary. I was very surprised that Otto and Anne had overheard this particular conversation."

2

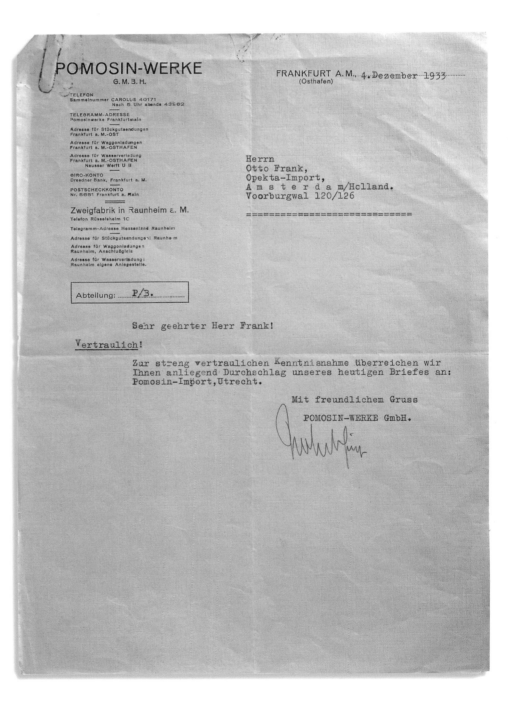

1 In the summer of 1944, twenty-four crates of strawberries are delivered to the office. The people in hiding are recruited to make jam in the office kitchen. *"That very same evening we immediately canned the first six jars and made eight pots of jam."* The following afternoon everybody has to help out.

"At twelve-thirty, outside door locked, crates fetched. Peter, Father, Van Pels clatter up the stairs, 'Anne, get warm water from the water heater! Margot, get a bucket! All hands on deck!' With an extremely weird feeling in my stomach I went into the overcrowded office kitchen – Miep, Bep, Kleiman, Jan, Father, Peter – those of us in hiding and our supply corps – all of us together and in the middle of the day too! The curtains and windows open, loud voices, banging doors; I was shaking from all the excitement. Okay, but are we still really in hiding? It flashed

1

3

through my mind that this must be how it feels when you can finally go out into the world again." (July 8, 1944)

In the evenings the people in hiding sometimes go to get warm water from the kitchen. There are curtains hanging so they can't be seen from the garden side.

"I went downstairs all by myself and looked out through the windows of the private office and kitchen. I'm not imagining it when I say that looking up at the sky, the clouds, the moon, and the stars makes me feel calm and hopeful. It's better medicine than either valerian or bromide; nature makes me feel humble and ready to take each blow with courage. Just my luck that except for rare occasions, I'm only able to gaze at nature through very dirty windows with dusty curtains hanging in front of them." (June 13, 1944)

3 "Just a short notation. Today I took a bath; it was rather strange. Picture this: I dragged a small washtub to the spacious office bathroom downstairs, then I filled it with hot water from the water heater in the office kitchen next door, I put my feet in it, meanwhile I'm sitting on the toilet trying to wash myself and of course the water's splashing everywhere and later, when I'm clean, I have to mop it all up again with the dirty mop." (September 27, 1942)

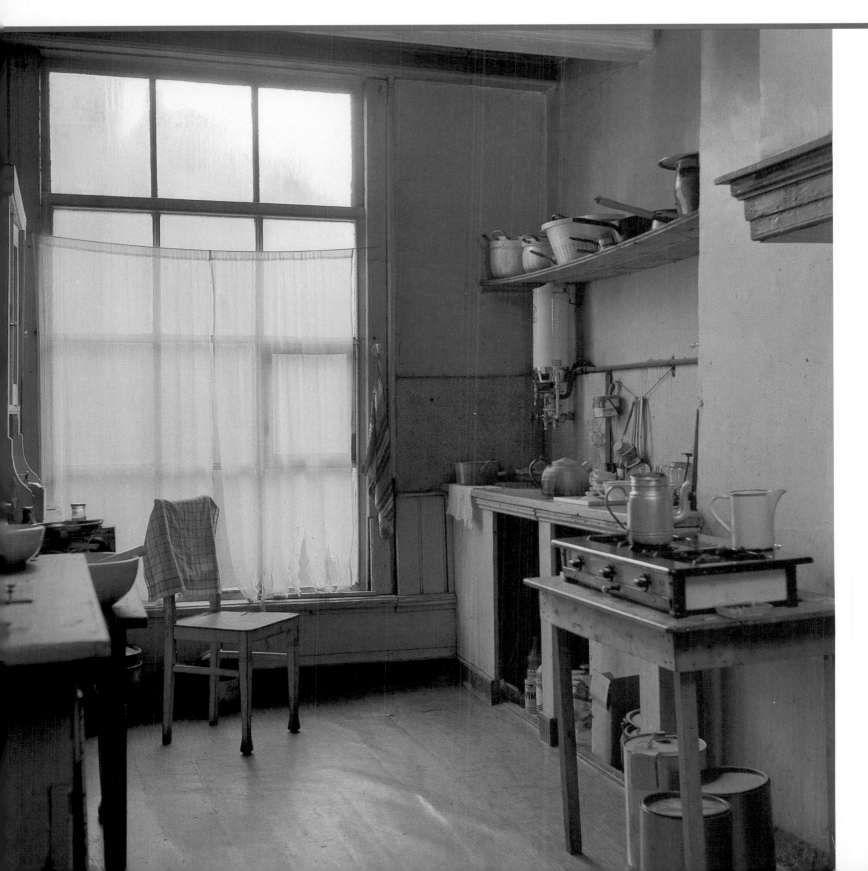

"From the big front office via an office supply room containing a safe, a wardrobe, and a big storage cupboard, you come to the small, dark, stuffy back office. This used to be shared by Mr. Kugler and Mr. van Pels, but now it is only from Mr. Kugler."

July 9, 1942

Victor Kugler's Office

Prior to the hiding period, Victor Kugler shared this office with Hermann van Pels.

During the hiding period Victor Kugler works here alone. He funnels money from

the business to those in hiding and furthermore feels responsible for their safety.

Kugler's office can only be reached via the front office and a door in the hallway,

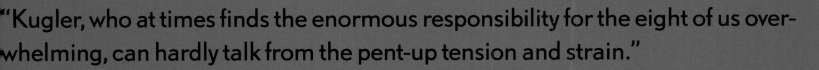

"Kugler, who at times finds the enormous responsibility for the eight of us over-whelming, can hardly talk from the pent-up tension and strain."

May 26, 1944

which can only be opened from the inside. Thus people entering from street

level cannot simply walk directly through the hall to the staircase that leads to

the hiding place. On the weekends and in the evenings the people in hiding,

and Fritz Pfeffer in particular, use this office as a writing room.

1 Victor Kugler at his desk in 1941. He is primarily responsible for the spice department of the business. In the afternoons, he and the other helpers go and eat lunch with the people in hiding.

On December 5, 1942, the helpers hide the *Sinterklaas** gifts for the inhabitants of the Secret Annex in the small office supply room located between Kugler's office and the front office. A few days later Anne writes about this surprise, and about the Jewish Chanukah festival that has just passed: *"Chanukah and St. Nicholas fell almost together this year, the difference was only one day. We didn't make much of a fuss about Chanukah. We exchanged some small gifts and then lit the candles. The Saturday evening of St. Nicholas was much nicer. Bep and Miep had aroused our curiosity by whispering to Father throughout dinner, so of course we suspected that something was up."* (December 7, 1942)

(* Feast of St. Nicholas: celebrated with sweets & gifts accompanied by candid & funny rhymes written for family & friends.)

*"At eight o'clock we all trooped down the wooden staircase, through the passage in pitch-darkness (It gave me the shivers and I wished that I was safely back upstairs again!) into the office supply room where we could switch on the lights because this room doesn't have windows. Once that was done Father opened the large closet. 'Oh, how nice,' we all yelled. A large basket decorated with St. Nicholas wrapping paper stood in the corner and there was a Pietmombakkes** attached to the top of it. We quickly took the basket upstairs. Inside was a little gift for each of us accompanied by an appropriate poem."* (December 7, 1942)
(* A cutout or mask of *Zwarte Piet* – literally 'Black Peter' – one of St. Nicholas' Moor helpers.)

2 Each week Victor Kugler brings the people in hiding different magazines and newspapers like: *De Prins* (The Prince), *Het Rijk der Vrouw* (Women's World), *De Haagse Post* (The Hague Post), and sometimes the German publication *Das Reich* (The Third Reich). Anne especially looks forward to the magazine *Cinema & Theater.* *"Mr. Kugler makes me happy every Monday when he brings Cinema & Theater magazine along with him. Though this small indulgence is often seen as a waste of money by the less worldly members of the household, they never fail to be amazed at how accurately I can name the actors in any given movie, even after a year."* (January 28, 1944)

3 At times during the hiding period, Anne helps with the work in Kugler's office. Sometimes she takes a bit of shorthand; other times she does some general office work. She writes in her diary in shorthand: *"...I'm really*

proud of myself that I can actually do this, because probably there aren't very many school children in the 2nd grade who can take shorthand… When I look at Bep's shorthand notebook I can't imagine how anybody can read such a mess, but apparently she knows what she's doing. Written in Kugler's office, with a window open, on Sunday, May 2, 1943."

"On Thursday night I was downstairs with Father drawing up the debtor's lists in Kugler's office. It was very creepy down there, and I was glad when the work was finished." (November 7, 1942)

"What else could I do? I had to help them; they were my friends," Victor Kugler says after the war. "I didn't tell my wife anything because she was very sick. I didn't want to worry her and so I couldn't talk about it at home. Life changed completely for the people in hiding. They had to remain completely silent, especially during the day. But it was also a tense and frightening time for us, the helpers. Our greatest fear was that the hiding place would be discovered. I had to put on an act for Otto Frank's former business associates, for clients and for the neighbors. Yet day-to-day life inside the Secret Annex as well as outside just continued along. Anne's probing eyes always looking at me as if to ask: 'Did you bring me *Cinema & Theater*? You know I'm crazy about it.' Sometimes I hid the magazine in my pocket just so I could look at those inquisitive eyes of hers a bit longer. When I was busy in my daily routine, I sometimes found it difficult to believe that two years had already passed. Their only chance for a better future was the Secret Annex, where they attempted to survive the storm. They had hoped to emerge from this hiding place once again as free people."

Victor Kugler around 1950

"This is the big front office — very large, very light and very full. Bep, Miep, and Mr. Kleiman work there during the day."

July 9, 1942

The Front Office of Miep Gies, Jo Kleiman, and Bep Voskuijl

The front office is run by three people: Miep Gies, Jo Kleiman, and Bep Voskuijl. They are all indispensable for the assistance they provide to those in hiding. During the day the work must continue as normally as possible. The office personnel arrives at nine in the morning. The warehousemen downstairs have then been working since eight-thirty. In that half-hour the people in hiding must remain completely quiet. Not a sound must be detected. Once the office personnel arrives it becomes less of a problem. They know about what's happening, and

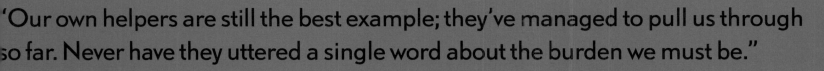

'Our own helpers are still the best example; they've managed to pull us through so far. Never have they uttered a single word about the burden we must be."

January 28, 1944

he warehousemen can think that the noise originates from the office. Yet, those in hiding have to continually be as quiet as possible because traveling salesmen do come to the office. The helpers are also always on their guard. At five-thirty in the evening the helpers give the "all-clear" signal through to the Secret Annex. After hours and in the weekends those in hiding also use this front office.

1 The office personnel in 1941, the year before going into hiding. From left to right: Victor Kugler (sitting at Jo Kleiman's desk), Esther, Bep Voskuijl, Pine, and Miep Gies. The last names of Esther and Pine are not known. In 1942 they are no longer employed.

2 On this machine Miep Gies types, for instance, letters for Opekta's "Helpful Hints" service. These include instructions about how to make jam using Opekta. Kugler also uses this typewriter for writing German business letters. In the evenings Otto Frank often takes the diverse typewriters up to the Secret Annex to prevent theft: *"Pim (Father) drags the typewriters upstairs,"* Anne reports on August 10, 1943.

"Every day all of them come upstairs and talk to the men about business and politics, to the women about food and wartime difficulties, to the children about books and newspapers. They manage to put on cheerful faces, bring flowers and presents for birthdays and holidays, and are always ready to do anything for us. That is what we should never forget, that although others exhibit heroism in battle or by standing up to the Germans, our helpers prove their heroism with their good spirits and devotion." (January 28, 1944)

3 The office personnel pass instructions to Opekta's sale representatives through this small window.

"Miep and Kugler bear the greatest burden for us, and for all those in hiding. Kleiman and Bep also take very good care of us, but they're able to put the Secret Annex out of their minds, even if it's only for a few hours, a day, perhaps two days. They have their own problems, Kleiman with his health, Bep with her engagement which apparently isn't going too well.

"Besides these worries, they also have their outings, their visits, their everyday lives as normal people."
(May 26, 1944)

Otto Frank and the four helpers. From left to right: Miep Gies, Jo Kleiman, Otto Frank, Victor Kugler, and Bep Voskuijl. The photo is taken after the war, probably by Kugler using the camera's self-timer.

3

4

2

1 Miep Gies does the daily grocery shopping together with Bep Voskuijl. She never knows what will be available: *"Every day the stores seemed emptier and the lines seemed longer."* What's more, Miep brings five library books along every Saturday and she keeps those in hiding abreast of the news from the outside world. Initially she relates everything about the razzias on the street, but when she realizes how disheartening this is to the inhabitants of the Secret Annex she keeps this information to herself.

'"Miep has so much to carry she looks like a pack mule. She goes forth nearly every day to scrounge up vegetables, and then bicycles back with her purchases in large shopping bags. We always long for Saturdays, because then the books arrive. We're like little children receiving a present. Normal people simply don't know how much meaning books can have for people shut away. Reading, learning, and the radio are our only distractions." (July 11, 1943)

2 The green grocer's shop at 58 Leliegracht with Riek van Hoeve standing in the doorway, circa 1940. Miep has reliable addresses for vegetables and meat. Henk van Hoeve, the vegetable man, knows about those in hiding and delivers without requesting ration coupons and at a normal price.

3 Henk van Hoeve is arrested on May 25, 1944 for hiding two Jews in his own home. He survives four concentration camps. The portrait photograph is taken shortly after his return from the camps.

4 During the Occupation all sorts of goods are rationed so that everybody can buy a bit of these scarce products. Along with the normal payment, store customers are also obliged to hand-in ration coupons. To get these coupons people have to present a "food rations card" at an allocation center. Obviously people in hiding, with a clandestine existence, don't have access to such a card. The Resistance sees to false documents. Miep's husband Jan Gies arranges the ration cards for the people hiding in the Secret Annex.

5 The identity card of Jan Gies. The German occupier requires all residents of the Netherlands to carry an identity card with them at all times. The cards of Jews are stamped with a large letter *J*.

6 The identity card of Miep Gies-Santrouschitz.

"Miep and Jan spent the night with us. Margot and I slept in Father and Mother's room for one night so the Gieses could have our beds. The honorary menu tasted

5

6

2

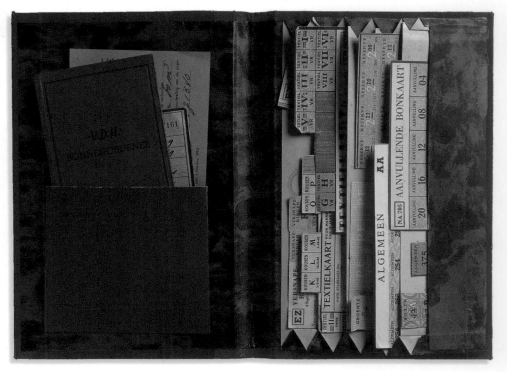

delicious. Following a pleasant breakfast Miep headed downstairs. It was pouring outside and she was glad she didn't have to ride to work on the bicycle."
(October 20, 1942)

Miep Gies in 1996

"I helped because I know how easily people find themselves in trouble without having done anything wrong," Miep says in 1998. "I couldn't save them, but at least I helped them. We didn't understand the word afraid, but later I sometimes thought: and now what? During the day we didn't talk much about the people in hiding. Everything had to proceed as normally as possible and it became too stressful if you discussed it. We had to appear as relaxed as possible to the outside world. Sometimes I lay awake at night thinking: oh, those people, that are hiding there, how awful. How would I feel? Well, I slept there one night and then I knew it. It was claustrophobic, terribly claustrophobic! It was basically the being locked away, the fact that you weren't allowed to go outside. True, it was wartime for all of us, but Jan and I were free to choose – to stay inside or to go out. These people were in prison, a prison where the doors were locked from the inside."

In a radio interview after the war, Kleiman says: "The reason I offered to help Otto Frank and his family during the hiding period, is because I knew him as a sincere businessman and a very decent and helpful person, qualities for which he is generally respected." Kleiman begins helping in the preparatory phase: "A few months before going into hiding we furnished the Secret Annex as a residence, where they could survive relatively well. The people in hiding could use the entire building after five-thirty in the evening. Looking outside wasn't so easy, because we hung up thick curtains everywhere. I didn't know that Anne wrote so much in her diary, and also about us – the helpers. I told my wife everything during the hiding period, but at first we didn't tell my daughter anything. Though at a certain moment I slipped, and then it seemed that she did know after all. Anne was thirteen when she came here and fifteen when she was taken away. In those two years she went from being a child to being a young woman."

Jo Kleiman in 1945

"Luckily Mr. Kleiman is around," Anne frequently writes with relief in her diary. No matter the situation, Jo Kleiman is the person that the people in hiding can always count on. He and is brother even help during the preparations for going into hiding. Otto Frank discusses all business affairs with him. Kleiman keeps in contact with Opekta's license holder in Basel – Erich Elias, the brother-in-law of Otto and Edith Frank. By calamities such as break-ins, a flea infestation, or an unexpected visitor, Kleiman is the first one to size up the situation. Also, according to Anne: *"he is a fantastic source of the latest citywide gossip."*

1 A certificate from the Trade Registry of the Chamber of Commerce. From December 16, 1941, Otto Frank's companies are registered under the names of the helpers. *"Mr. Kleiman has taken over Opekta and Mr. Kugler, Gies & Co., the firm in spice substitutes,"*

Anne writes in her diary on July 5, 1942. In day-to-day practice, Otto Frank still remains the boss. During the hiding period Kleiman and Kugler consult with him on a daily basis.

The label design for bottles of pectin used in making jam and jelly.

So Kleiman's (on the left) recurring illness is a continuous worry. In 1943 and 1944 he struggles with his stomach. When he's feeling better, he comes to the office as much as possible.

"The stomach ulcers of Mr. Kleiman, who always tries to cheer us up, started hemorrhaging yesterday and he has to stay in bed for at least three weeks. You should know that he suffers a lot with bleeding ulcers, and there doesn't seem be any cure." (April 1, 1943)

4 *"Every other week Mr. Kleiman brings me a few books written for girls my age, he's so nice, he brings everything right on schedule,"* Anne writes on September 21, 1942. Kleiman also surprises her with *The Young People's Annual.* Later he brings books to Anne and Margot that his daughter has finished reading. Sometimes he comes to the Secret Annex with his wife. Anne then asks Mrs. Kleiman everything there is to know about the life of her daughter and the outside world.

"I've written a lot about how much the atmosphere here affects our moods and I think that in my case this affliction is getting much worse lately. 'Himmelhoch jauchzend, zu Tode betrubt', ('On top of the world, or in the depths of despair') certainly applies to me. I am 'Himmelhoch jauchzend', if I think about how good we have it here and I compare myself to other

Jewish children and 'zu Tobe betrubt' *comes over me for example when Mrs. Kleiman has been here and tells us about Jopie's hockey club, canoe trips, school plays, and tea parties with friends."*
(December 24, 1943)

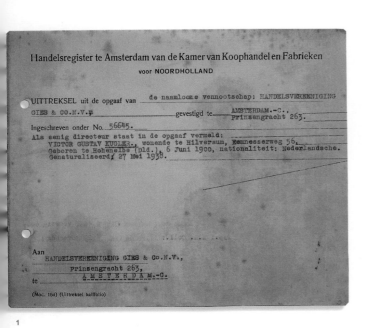

1

4

2

1 Bep Voskuijl (left) with her office colleages, Miep, Esther, and Pine in front of the building on the Prinsengracht, 1941. Bep, together with Miep Gies, is responsible for the food provisions. She is the oldest child of a family with six children. Her full name is Elisabeth, but mostly she is called Bep. Because there isn't enough for everyone to eat at home she eats her daily meal with those in hiding. Just like Miep and Jan, Bep also spends a night (October 30, 1942) in the Secret Annex. At home the Voskuijl family does not discuss the people in hiding, still both the father and also sister Corry help out. Father Voskuijl builds the bookcase and Corry, a seamstress, makes clothing for Anne and Margot.

2 Bep Voskuijl's identity card. Bep initially goes to work as a domestic and in a sewing workshop. She follows various evening courses to become a fully-qualified office-clerk. This profession is one of the few good professional opportunities for young women from blue-collar and middle-class families. It is considered schooled work and pays decently.

3 Front Office, 1940. From the left: Esther, Hermann van Pels, and Miep Gies, with Bep Voskuijl in the foreground.

"Isn't a member of the Secret Annex family, although she does share our house and table. Bep has a healthy appetite, doesn't leave anything over, and isn't picky. It's easy to please her and that pleases us. Cheerful and good-humored, cooperative and kind – those are her qualities." (August 9, 1943)

"Bep almost had a nervous breakdown this week because she had to do so many errands. Ten times a day people were sending her out for something, each time insisting that she go right away or go again or that she'd done it wrong. If you just think that she still has to finish her office work downstairs, that Kleiman is ill, Miep is at home with a cold, and that Bep herself has a sprained ankle, boyfriend troubles, and a grumpy father at home, then it's no wonder that she's at her wits end." (September 29,1943)

"Bep has ordered some association's correspondence course in shorthand for Margot, Peter, and me. I think it's really impressive to actually learn such a secret code." (October 1, 1942)

→ Sometimes Anne also writes a few lines in her diary in shorthand.

Following the war Bep Voskuijl keeps a scrapbook about Anne. It also contains a 1960 newspaper clipping of one of the few interviews given by Bep: "I ate dinner with the Franks every night. Anne always sat next to me and almost immediately she asked me if I would keep an eye open for a sturdy hardcover notebook where she could note down her daily experiences. It was a shame but in all of Amsterdam I couldn't find such a thing and I therefore gave Anne some blank loose-leaf pages. The child was delighted with this. Once I stayed and slept in the Secret Annex. Honestly speaking, I was terribly frightened. When I heard a tree creaking or when a car drove along the canal, I became frightened. I was thankful when the morning came and I could once again just return to my work. I can still see Anne crouching here under my desk trying to get a glimpse of the outside world, the street, the canal. Naturally we had to be careful because nobody was supposed to know that there were other people in this building besides the bunch of us in the office."

Bep van Wijk-Voskuijl
around 1960

Beste Pop...
Allweer 2 ...
delijk. Rosel...
waarom da...
Miep gaat...
het goed v...
wat in ste...
gevraagd ...
Lig. Moeder...
maatjes, da...
"lig nu bijna
hebben er o...
zorgster...
vak, maar
plaats v...
Ook wel ee...
krijgt, wan...
me zelf. Ma...
maar dat z...
2 broers en...
Was nog een...
Mijnh. v. Pel...
ik zalze hier...
Wie doet 999...

de andere kant, een meneer.
De mannelijke heeft van het
paartje klopt het vrouwelijke
steeds op zijn achterste terwijl hij zegt:, Ach was ein schö-
nes popöchen, von wem, ist den
das schöne popöchen? Daar roept
de man aan de andere kant:
"Es wird sich doch noch raus-
stellen lassen, von wem das
verdamte asch ist!

Ze zijn wel goed hé! Beste Pop
Veel nieuws is er niet meer,
en ik vind altijd dat als ik de
brieven doorlees er niets
leuks instaat dusdaag, ik hoop
dat ik spoedig bericht krijg.
            Annefrank

Steno.
C ... U ... S C U = de hal lil op
de hak.
... G ... = ik moes mel de
                hen.

...rdag
...och sch
...ehaald
...elukkig
...teno ga
...ien ee
...Ber
...gel
...beste
...iger. Ik
...We
...raam Ve
...en Lijn
...ers in
...r toch
...ind
...eng vo
...kouden
...s is m
...d, dat
...e lang.
...vertel

Wie doet 999 maal tik en 1 maal tak?
Een 1000 poot met 1 klompvoet.
Wie is zwart, zit op het dak, heeft twee poten en
kan fluiten?
De leerling van den schoorsteenmeester.
            (Papi)
In een hotel zijn de muren net als bij ons bete...
geld, en daar kan men dus alles door horen. Op een
...eet is aan de ene kant een paartje en a...

h. "Fräulein es blitst!"
. "Licht mam?."
. "ag!"

h. "Nein, nur der Unterrock!"

_____

de oorlog gauw afgelopen is. Mijnh.
ler heeft weer 12 Panorama's mee-
racht, nu hebben we weer wat te lezen.
ep was bij mevr. Stoppelman het arme
ns houdt het niet uit in haar schuil-
ts van heimwee en honger. Bep heeft
het groenten winkeltje waar ze altijd koopt,
Vroeger meisje van de Tokita ont-
t met haar kind van 3 jaar. Ik vroeg
ect. is die dan getrouwd, dat was na-
urlijk niet het geval, en men neemt
, dat het het zoveelste kind van Ro-
hdael is. Schandalig, wat een man.
p heeft van iemand verteld die uit
sterbork gevlucht is, nou het is daar
schrikkelijk, en als het daar al zo
g is hoe moet het dan wel in Polen
n) De mensen krijgen haast niets te eten
t at aan drinken, want ze hebben maar
ur per dag water en 1 w.c. en 1 was-tafel
r een paar 1000 mensen. Slapen doen ze
maal door elkaar mannen en vrouwen
die laatste + kinderen krijgen vaak de
ren afgeschoren, als ze dan vluchten
n iedereen zeker kennen. Anne Frank.

te vragen

Evenings and in the weekends, when the business is closed down, the people in hiding often come out of the hiding place. Sometimes they come to the front office, where the thick curtains are drawn closed after business hours. For Anne, who is dying for a glimpse of the outside world, this is a thrilling room.

"Margot and I have declared the front office to be our bathing grounds. Since the curtains are drawn on Saturday afternoon, we scrub ourselves in the dark, while the one who isn't in the bath looks out the window through a chink in the curtains, and gazes in wonder at the endlessly amusing people."

September 29, 1942

"I'm sitting cozily in the front office looking outside through a chink in the heavy curtains. It's dusk, but still just light enough to write. It's really strange watching people walking by, it seems as if they're all in a terrible hurry and are practically tripping over their own feet. The bicycles whiz by so fast that I can't even tell what sort of person is riding the thing."

December 13, 1942

"The people in this neighborhood aren't so very attractive and the children in particular are so dirty you wouldn't want to touch them with a ten-foot pole – real slum kids with runny noses. I can hardly understand a word they say. Yesterday afternoon Margot and I were taking a bath here and I said: 'If we took a fishing rod and reeled in each of those kids one by one as they walked by, put them in a bath, washed and mended their clothes, and then let them go again, then...' To this Margot replied: 'And then tomorrow, they'd be just as filthy and look just as ragged as before.'"

December 13, 1942

As if I'd seen one of the World Wonders, I saw two Jews through the curtain yesterday, it
was a horrible feeling, just as if I had betrayed them to the authorities and was now watching
them in their misery."

December 13, 1942

The women always put the bread in the kitchen cupboard but it's not there: someone's
forgotten. Peter wants to look in the front office. He crawls on his hands and knees to the
steel cabinet, takes out the bread and wants to get out of there, but before he realizes it,
Mouschi has jumped over him. Peter looks all around him, aha, there's the cat. He crawls
back into the office and grabs the beast by its tail. Mouschi hisses, Peter sighs. Mouschi is
now sitting all the way by the window licking herself, quite pleased to have escaped Peter's
clutches. In a last ditch attempt Peter now waves a piece of bread in front of the cat, and yes!
Mouschi falls for the bait and the door is closed."

August 10, 1943

"Hiding, where would we hide? In the city? In the country? In a house?
In a shack, when, where, how ...?"

July 8, 1942

The Storeroom

The third floor of the front part of the house is used for storage during the war

years. The spices are stockpiled in the rear of the space. To protect them from

the light the windows are covered over with blue paint. This also keeps the

hiding place from being discovered by outsiders who might come to this floor.

Anne Frank hears the news about the ongoing persecution of the Jews from

'Countless friends and acquaintances have been taken off to a dreadful fate. Night after night, green and gray military vehicles cruise the streets. It's impossible to escape their clutches unless you go into hiding."

November 19, 1942

he helpers, the radio, and Fritz Pfeffer – a later arrival to the Secret Annex.

She describes these accounts in her diary. Step-by-step, Nazi-Germany forces

the Jews of Europe into a corner. Under the guise of "labor camps", the Nazis

deport large numbers of Jews "to the East". The exact destination is kept secret,

just like the true nature of these so-called labor camps.

94

Sonja Souget
in 1999

As it happens, Sonja Souget almost escapes the razzia by passing for "Aryan". Her childhood maid helps by claiming to be her mother. The razzia occurs shortly before her "Aryanization" is completed, Sonja has all the "Aryanization papers" in her handbag. "A lot of storm troopers (SS) were deployed on May 26th, and all of them hauled people out of their homes. They rang doorbells, they banged on front doors, they came inside and looked under the beds, next to the beds, behind the beds, in the closets. Everywhere you looked there were soldiers. We were surrounded, we couldn't escape. Otherwise, I surely would have done this. I had the nerve, but it came as a complete surprise." Sonja is detained in a nearby synagogue, together with other apprehended Jews. She is freed thanks to a concocted story, and a short time later she does receive a new, non-Jewish, identity card. This enables her to escape further persecution.

1 The storeroom in 1954. During the war years Opekta's mixing barrels are kept here. All sorts of packing good and raw materials are also stored here. The people in hiding basically never come here, not even in the evenings.

"It's like the slave hunts of long ago. In the evenings when it's dark, I often see long lines of good, innocent people, walking with crying children, walking on and on, ordered about by a handful of men who bully and beat them until they nearly drop. Nobody is spared – the elderly, children, babies, expectant mothers, the sick – all are marched to their deaths." (November 19, 1942)

2 Awaiting the deportation transport at Amsterdam's Muiderpoort train station, May 25, 1943.

nne's heart goes out to the Jews who are picked up. he also thinks of her former school friend Hannah Goslar. *"I saw her standing in front of me, dressed in ags, her face thin and worn. Yet, I can't help her. I can nly stand by and watch while other people suffer and ie. All I can do is pray to God to bring her back to us."* November 27, 1943)

If we just wouldn't worry about those who were so ear to us, whom we can no longer help. I feel awful leeping in a warm bed, while my dearest friends are ut there somewhere being knocked to the ground r dropping from exhaustion. I get frightened myself hen I think of all of them, the friends I felt so bound , who are now at the mercy of the cruelest monsters ver to stalk the earth. And all because they're Jews." November 19, 1942)

3 One of the few photos made of a razzia in Amsterdam. It is early in the morning on May 26, 1943. The center of Amsterdam is surrounded. Three thousand Jews are removed from their homes. They are taken by train to Westerbork and from there transported to one of the extermination camps. The pharmacist on Geldersekade snaps a photograph of his neighbors being led away. The woman walking past the lamppost is Sonja Souget.

4 A note thrown from a deportation train as a plea for help. *"December 17, 1943. Sister, help me. I'm being taken to Westerbork, for God's sake help me quickly, kiss my loved ones, Meta."* At the end of 1943, Sonja Souget receives this note from her sister who is later murdered in Sobibor.

3

2

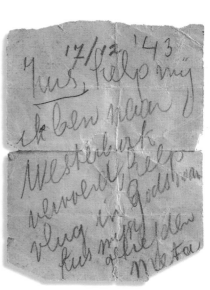

4

1 Apprehended Jews awaiting transport to Westerbork, 1942. On October 3rd of that year Anne writes: *"Once again this morning Miep told us that last night they went door to door again picking up Jews in the South (of Amsterdam). It's impossible to imagine how terrible it is. I'm just so happy we're here."* Massive razzias occur throughout the Netherlands on the 2nd and 3rd of October 1942. By the end of 1942, 40,000 of the Jews living in the Netherlands have been deported.

2 Amsterdam, April 1943. This streetcar is taking Jews to Muiderpoort train station. From there they will be deported further, to Westerbork transit camp. An armed German soldier is standing on the footboard. Transports are usually carried out early in the morning, yet many bystanders still witness the deportations. In Amsterdam the last mass razzias occur in 1943, on June 20th and September 29th. Of the 140,000

Jews in the Netherlands, 107,000 are deported. Only 5,000 of them will survive the camps.

"Miep's accounts of these horrors are so heartrending, and she is also very distraught. The other day, for instance, the Gestapo deposited an elderly, crippled Jewish woman on Miep's doorstep while they set off to find a car to take her away. The old woman was so terrified of the loud guns firing at the English planes overhead and also of the glaring searchlights. Yet Miep didn't dare to let her in, nobody would do that. The Germans are generous enough when it comes to punishment." (October 9, 1942)

"Going underground or into hiding has simply become routine and you cannot imagine how much is done by organizations such as "The Free Netherlands". Thousands and thousands of identity

1

2

3

nd ration cards are being provided, sometimes for
nothing and sometimes for money. Just how many
alse identity cards are in circulation is anyone's
guess. Jewish acquaintances have taken on names
hat are commonly considered Christian and there
re certainly not many people in hiding like ourselves,
with no identity cards who never go out on the street."
(January 28, 1944)

A small percentage of Jews succeeds in evading arrest
nd deportation by means of, for example, taking on a
ifferent identity. These people are given or sold forged
dentity cards by the Resistance. This organization's
reach and resolve against the German occupying force
ncreases as the war progresses.

By the end of 1943, a majority of the Jewish population
as been deported. The Nazis intensify their efforts to

arrest Jews in hiding. Considerable rewards are offered
to those who betray Jews. This receipt, dated April 6,
1943, is for thirty-seven guilders and fifty cents paid
to someone for betraying five Jews. Although somewhere in the neighborhood of 25,000 Jews go into
hiding in the Netherlands, 8,000 are still caught due
to betrayals.

5   In 1948, Victor Kugler testifies that he once came
across Van Maaren, the warehouseman, in the storeroom: *"To block the view of the so-called Secret Annex
we had daubed several windows in the rear of the
front part of the house with blue paint, supposedly
for blackout purposes. On one particular occasion
I caught Van Maaren in the act of scratching away
some of the blue paint on a window and he reacted
by saying: 'Hey, I've never been over there.'"* It appears
from Anne's diary that this storage space was not only

used for spices and other company articles, but also for
storing food for the people in hiding: *"Besides, we still
have about 230 pounds of winter potatoes in the rear
of the spice storeroom."* (February 3, 1944)

"A wooden staircase leads from the downstairs passage to the next floor. At the top of the stairs is a landing, with doors on either side. The right-hand door leads to the 'Secret Annex'."

July 9, 1942

The Movable Bookcase

Once the Frank family and the Van Pels family have been in hiding for more than a month, a decision is made to camouflage the entry door to the Annex. To do this, the stoop leading up to the Annex's gray door needs to be removed and then the door itself can be lowered. The warehouse manager Voskuijl builds the movable bookcase. The short staircase opening onto the landing in front of the bookcase

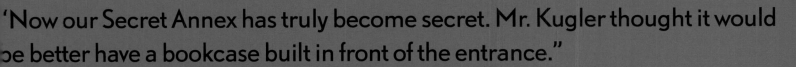

"Now our Secret Annex has truly become secret. Mr. Kugler thought it would
be better have a bookcase built in front of the entrance."

August 21, 1942

...eads down to the office spaces on the second floor. The helpers use this stairway

when they visit the Secret Annex. In the evenings and on weekends, when the

people in hiding come out of the Secret Annex, they descend this staircase to get

to the offices below.

On July 6, 1942, when the people in hiding first arrive at the Annex there is just an ordinary door on this spot. You enter the Annex by way of a few steps. Anne writes: *"No one would ever suspect that there could be so many rooms hidden behind that plain gray-painted door. There's just a small stoop going up to the door, and then you're inside."* (July 9, 1942)

Victor Kugler hits on the idea of making a movable bookcase to conceal the entranceway.

"Mr. Voskuijl has finished building the contraption; before doing that the walls of the landing had to be papered. Now whenever we want to go downstairs we have to duck and then jump. After three days we were all walking around with foreheads full of lumps from bumping our heads against the lowered doorway. Then Peter made it as soft as possible by nailing a piece of cloth filled with wood-wool to it. Let's see if that helps!" (August 21, 1942)

1 Due to the removal of two treads one has to take a step of more than 1½ feet to enter the Annex.

2 A panel is used to board-up the opening at the top of the doorway. A map is hung in front of that panel. The panel, covering the opening created by lowering the door, is still visible today.

3 After the war, Kleiman explains how the helpers opened the entrance to the hiding place from the outside. By pulling on a cord hanging next to the bookcase the helpers are able to unlatch the hook and then the bookcase can be swung open. With a handle, the people in hiding can pull the door closed from the inside and latch it once again. Hanging on the bookcase is the same piece of cloth filled with wood-wool that Peter once nailed above the door.

4 This is a photo taken from the landing in the direction of the storeroom. One of the five Minimax appliances that Anne mentions in her diary can still be seen. At a certain moment a repairman comes to the building to service the five fire extinguishers. The people in hiding are not forewarned and suddenly hear hammering coming from the landing. They are completely terrified, as is Bep, who is upstairs in the Secret Annex eating a meal.

"Father and I stationed ourselves at the door so we could hear when the man was leaving. After working for about fifteen minutes, he put his hammer and other tools on our bookcase and banged on our door. We turned white – had he heard something after all

1

2

nd now wanted to check out this mysterious-looking
ontraption? It seemed so, since the knocking, pulling,
ushing and jerking on the bookcase continued.
nearly fainted from fright. And just when I thought
my days were numbered, we heard Mr. Kleiman's voice
aying: 'Open up, it's me.'" (October 20, 1942)

he same sort of Minimax fire extinguisher that is
epaired on October 20, 1942. The people in hiding
ear about what has happened from Jo Kleiman.
nne writes: *"The hook fastening the bookcase had
otten stuck, which is why no one could warn us about
he carpenter."* After the repairman has left, Kleiman
oes upstairs again to get Bep, but he can't open the
ookcase. *"I can't tell you how relieved I was. Whew!
Thank goodness everything worked out all right for
s this time."* (October 20, 1942)

4

3

In August 1942, at the request of the people in hiding, Johan Voskuijl, the father of the helper Bep, builds the movable bookcase. Willy, a younger sister of Bep, recalls: "We knew nothing about the Frank family being in hiding. What we did notice is that after dinner Bep and father often sat together talking very quietly." Johan Voskuijl is actually a bookkeeper by trade, but through Bep he comes to work for the firm Opekta as a warehouse manager. He is diagnosed with stomach cancer in 1937. Anne mentions his illness in her diary on several occasions. Bep Voskuijl writes to Otto Frank on March 21, 1951: "Anne was always so nice to me and empathized with my family, also when father was so sick she asked about him every day and once said: 'Listen, when we get out of here, Pim (Otto Frank) and I are going to visit your father first.'" Otto Frank is very fond of Johan Voskuijl. He is therefore pleasantly surprised when he returns from Auschwitz and sees that father Voskuijl is still alive. Unfortunately, Johan Voskuijl does not live much longer. He dies in November 1945.

Johan Voskuijl
around 1931

← A wooden staircase ascends from the floor where the offices are located to the landing in front of the movable bookcase. The helpers use this staircase when they want to go to the Secret Annex. *"Kugler comes up the stairs hurry-scurry, a short sturdy knock on the door and in he comes, wringing his hands in proportion to his mood, either good-tempered and boisterous or bad tempered and silent."* (August 5, 1943)

← Today, the stairwell is sealed-off with a piece of glass. During the hiding period a policeman unexpectedly comes up these stairs. It is April 8, 1944. Once again the company building has been broken into. The outside door has been damaged and a couple passing by has warned the police. The people in hiding huddle together on the uppermost floor afraid to move at all.

1

2

Then, at eleven-fifteen, a noise below. You could hear the whole family breathing hard, for the rest no one moved an inch. Footsteps in the house, the private office, the kitchen, then ... our staircase. Now everybody was holding their breath, eight hearts pounded. Footsteps on our stairs, then a rattling at the bookcase. This moment is indescribable. 'Now we're done for,' I said, and I had visions of all fifteen of us being dragged away by the Gestapo that very night. Rattling at the bookcase, twice, then we heard a can fall, the footsteps receded. So far, we were out of danger! A shiver went through everyone's body, I heard several sets of teeth chattering, no one said a word. We stayed like this until eleven-thirty." (April 11, 1944)

During the war years, a dense semitransparent paper (glassine) is affixed to the windows on the landing. Therefore the policeman cannot see the Secret Annex

and simply goes away again. Yet, the people in hiding are still very worried. "We then did three things: tried to guess what was going on, trembled with fear and needed to go to the toilet." (April 11, 1944) They don't dare to use the bathroom which is one floor below. They all spend a restless night together on the top floor.

2 Anne regularly writes about the tensions in the Secret Annex and the despondent moods of its inhabitants. Constantly feeling unsafe is just one of the reasons for this. Anne cannot conceive, for instance, that the warehouse employees never notice anything. As an outcome of the burglaries the people in hiding agree to new security measures. Everybody has to be back in the Secret Annex by 9:30 p.m. when the movable bookcase is shut.

"Peter and Mr. van Pels do a last check every night at nine-thirty and after that nobody's allowed downstairs.

We can't flush the toilet any more after eight at night, nor after eight o'clock in the morning. The windows may only be opened in the morning when the lights go on in Mr. Kugler's office, and they may no longer be propped open at night with a stick." (April 25, 1944)

2

"In papa and mama's room there were two divans and two small tables with a smoker's table and a small set of bookshelves. There were 150 cans of vegetables and all sorts of other supplies in the built-in cupboard."

July 8, 1942

Otto, Edith and Margot Frank's Room

Today the rooms of the Annex are empty. The furniture and remaining belongings of the people in hiding are carted away, by order of the German occupier, shortly after the arrest. In this space, the sitting-room of the Frank family, pencil marks recording the height of Anne and Margot and a map of Normandy can still be

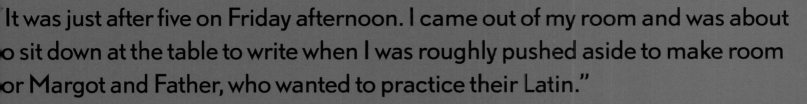

It was just after five on Friday afternoon. I came out of my room and was about o sit down at the table to write when I was roughly pushed aside to make room or Margot and Father, who wanted to practice their Latin."

November 11, 1943

een on the wall. The Frank family spends the major portion of the day here during he hiding period. After the arrival of Fritz Pfeffer, Margot sleeps in this room vith her parents. Sometimes the tensions among the family members run high, et there are also always reoccurrences of harmony.

1 When the Frank family arrives at the location of the hiding place, all the rooms are filled with furniture, boxes, and food supplies. Anne writes about that: *"Our living room and all the other rooms were so full of stuff that I can't find the words to describe it. All the cardboard boxes which had been sent to the office in the last few months were piled-up on the ground and on the beds."* (July 10, 1942)

"Mother and Margot were unable to move a muscle. They lay down on their bare mattresses, were tired, miserable and I don't know what else. But Father and I, the two cleaner-uppers in the family, wanted to begin straight away. All day long we unpacked boxes, filled cupboards, hammered nails and straightened up the mess, until we fell exhausted into our clean beds at night." (July 10, 1942)

2 The people in hiding must not move around during office hours. So this time is usually reserved for studying and reading. Anne: *"Quiet! The clock is striking! Now for a really close look at the picture-perfect family. I choose to read or study and Margot does too. Father and Mother, ditto. Father is sitting (with Dickens and the dictionary, of course) on the edge of the sagging, squeaky bed, which doesn't even have a proper mattress – piling two bolster pillows on top of each other does the trick. Mother sits on the folding bed, reading, sewing, knitting or studying, just whatever is next on her list."* (August 23, 1943)

3 *"We while away the time with all kinds of crazy activities: telling riddles, exercising in the dark, speaking English or French, reviewing books – eventually everything gets boring. Yesterday I discovered something new: using a good pair of binoculars to peek into the*

ghted rooms of the neighbors out back. During the ay our curtains can't be opened, not even an inch, ut there's no harm when it's dark. I never knew that eighbors could be such interesting people, anyway urs are. I've happened upon a few eating dinner, ne family had just begun shooting home movies, nd the dentist across the way was working on an old, rightened woman." (November 28, 1942)

Don't get me wrong. I still love Father as much as ver, and Margot loves both Father and Mother, but vhen you're as old as we are, you want to make a few ecisions for yourself, get out from under your parent's ule. If I go upstairs, they ask what I'm busy with. hey won't let me salt my food. Mother asks me every vening at 8:15 if it isn't time for me to change into my ajamas, and they have to approve every book I read." March 17, 1944)

→ Probably the last photo taken of Margot and Anne.

→ From the moment they go into hiding, Otto and Edith keep track of how much their daughters grow. In those two years Anne grows more than five inches and Margot around two inches.

On June 12, 1943, Anne celebrates her fourteenth birth-day. Her father gives her a special poem he's written in German, which Margot translates. A selection from Otto Frank's gift:

"The many months here have not been in vain
Since wasting time goes against your grain.
You read and study nearly all the day.
Determined to chase the boredom away.
The more difficult question, much harder to bear,
Is 'What on earth do I have to wear?

I've got no more panties, my clothes are too tight,
My shirt is a loincloth, I'm really a sight!
To put on my shoes I must cut off my toes,
Oh dear, I'm plagued with so many woes!'
Yes, if you grow four inches more,
Don't expect to wear what you wore before."
(June 13, 1943)

2

3

25-9
18-9

29-7

27-5

22-12

43 - 14-12

20-10

15-9 6-7

9-I

24-IX

— 25 III

22-II 9-III

— 10-1

10-2

2-12

18/10
25-9

— 1. 18-9-1912

1 On November 16, 1942, Margot starts sleeping in the same room as her parents on a folding bed that was previously kept upstairs in the attic. In the early months of hiding it's used by people for sunbathing in the attic, as Anne describes: *"It's a beautiful warm day outside, and in spite of everything we make the most of the weather by lounging on the folding bed in the attic, where the sun shines through an open window."* (August 21, 1942)

2 Margot, shortly before going into hiding, on the roof-terrace of the house on Merwedeplein. She is probably sitting on the same folding bed that she will later sleep on during the hiding period.

3 Margot Frank's report card from the Municipal High School for girls, summer 1941. Given her school achievements, it is not surprising that Margot is

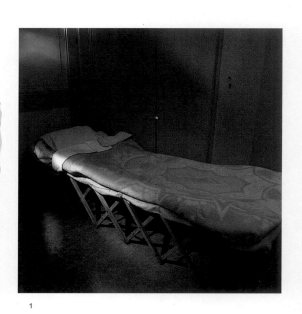

1

2

4

considered the "teacher" of the Secret Annex. he translates from German to Dutch and gives Dutch lessons to Fritz Pfeffer. Anne writes on August 5, 1943: "Margot tucks a few books under her arm and heads for the class for 'slow learners', which is what Pfeffer seems to be." In her diary Anne makes a list of the interests of those in hiding. Margot's list is the most extensive.

Margot Frank is learning: English and French; Latin via a correspondence course; shorthand in English, German and Dutch; trigonometry; solid geometry; mechanics; physics; chemistry; algebra; geometry; English, French, German and Dutch literature; bookkeeping; geography; modern history; biology; economics; reads everything, preferably about religion and medicine." (May 16, 1944)

4 Using her own name, Bep Voskuijl orders a Latin correspondence course for Margot. The teacher has no idea that a Jewish girl in hiding is doing the course. Anne says regarding this: *"Margot sends her Latin lessons to a teacher, who corrects and then returns them. She's registered under Bep's name. The teacher's very nice, and witty too. I bet he's glad to have such a smart student."* (November 17, 1943)

5 In addition to all the reading and studying she does, Margot, just like Anne, keeps a diary. This diary has never been found.

"Last night, Margot and I were lying side by side in my bed. It was incredibly cramped, but that's what made it fun. She asked if she could read my diary now and then. 'Parts of it,' I said, and then I asked about hers. She gave me permission to read her diary as well.

Then the conversation turned to the future and I asked her what she wanted to be when she was older, but she wouldn't say and was quite mysterious about it." (October 14, 1942) Later on Margot does tell Anne about her future plans. She wants to become a maternity nurse in Palestine.

"Margot is very kind and would like me to confide in her, but I can't tell her everything. She takes me too seriously, much too seriously, spends a lot of time trying to figure out her loony sister, looks at me curiously every time I open my mouth, wondering: is she joking or does she literally mean what she's saying?" (March 12, 1944)

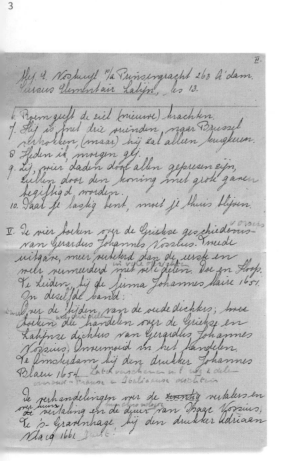

3

5

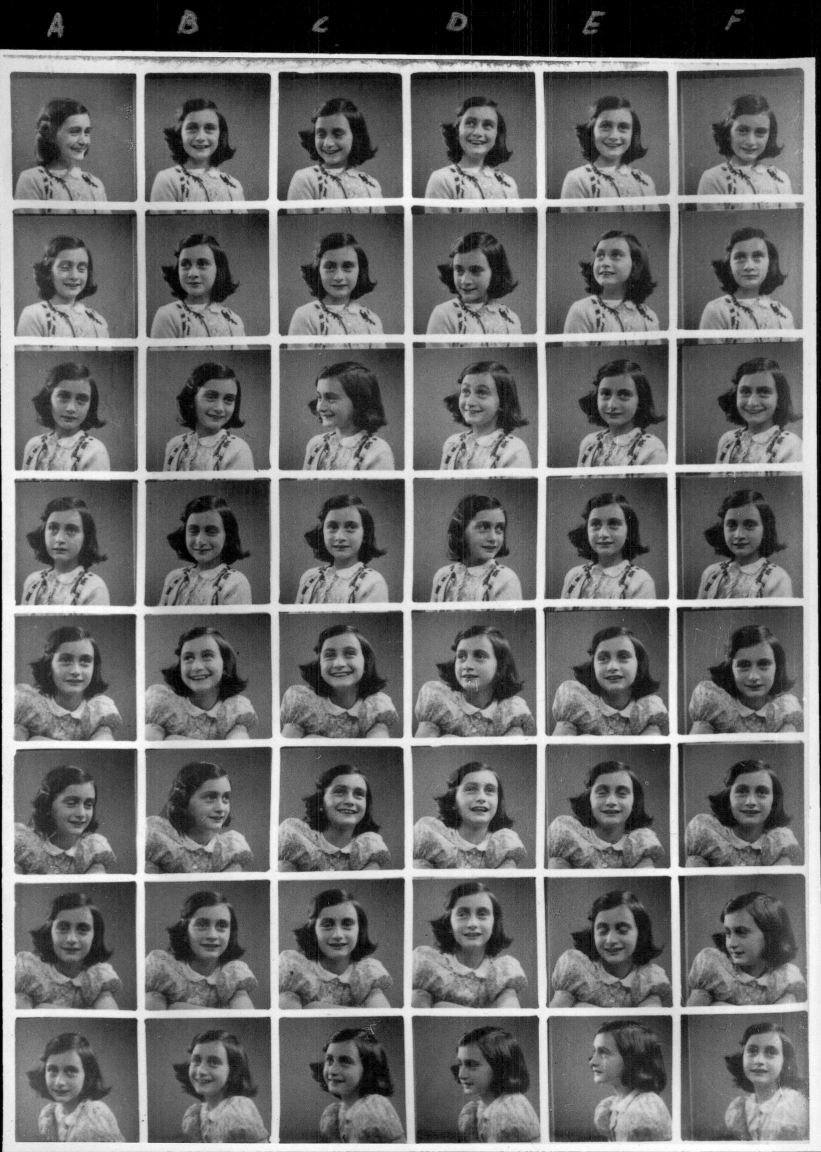

1 During the hiding period, Edith Frank keeps the various rooms in the Annex clean and does the dishes. In addition, she reads a lot and just like Margot, takes a correspondence course. Anne writes in her diary: *"Mrs. Frank: learns English by correspondence course; reads everything except detective stories."* (May 16, 1944)

2 Edith Frank is a religious woman. She tries to pass this on to her daughters but with no success, as Anne herself indicates: *"Father has taken the plays of Goethe and Schiller down from the big bookcase and is planning to read to me every evening. We've already started* Don Carlos. *Encouraged by Father's good example, Mother pressed her prayer book into my hands. I read a few prayers in German, just to be polite. They certainly sound beautiful, but don't mean very much to me. Why is she always pushing me to behave so saintly and devout?"* (October 29, 1942)

"Last night I was lying in bed waiting for Father to tuck me in and say my prayers with me, when Mother came into the room, sat on my bed and asked very hesitantly: 'Anne, Daddy isn't quite ready. Why don't we pray together?' 'No, Moms,'* I replied. Mother got up, stood beside my bed for a moment and then slowly walked toward the door. Suddenly she turned around, her face contorted with pain, and said: 'I don't want to be angry with you. You can't force love!' A few tears slid down her cheeks as she went out the door." (April 2, 1943) (* See diary: December 24, 1943. Anne addresses her mother as "Moms" to emphasize that she's the "imperfect Mommy". Anne feels this represents how incomplete their relationship is.)

Each of the sisters has a different kind of relationship with their parents. Margot is much closer to her mother than Anne: *"I think Mother believes that Margot and I have a better relationship with our parents than anyone in the whole wide world, and that no mother is more involved in the lives of her children than she is. With this she certainly only takes Margot into account, because I don't believe she ever has the same problems and thoughts as I do. Mother does sense that Margot loves her much more than I do, but she thinks I'm just going through a phase."* (January 12, 1944)

3 Edith Frank finds being in hiding very difficult. She does not get along with the Van Pels family and is pessimistic about the future. In spite of her gloominess she still makes plans for after the war. According to Miep Gies, Edith, just like her eldest daughter, wanted to go to Palestine. In the eyes of her youngest daughter, Edith cannot do much of anything right. Anne sees her only as an example of how *not* to do things.

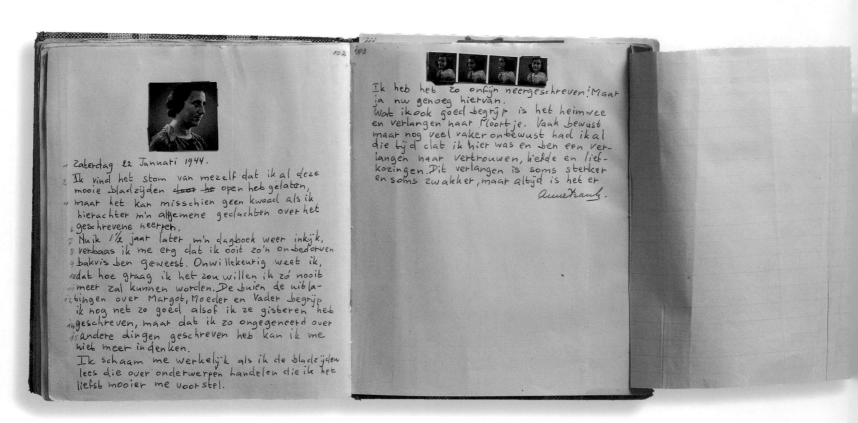

3

2

"Mother has said that she sees us more as friends than daughters. That's all very nice, of course, but still a friend can't take a mother's place. I need my mother to set a good example and be a person I can respect. And in most matters my mother does set an example for me, but precisely an example of how I shouldn't do it! I have the feeling that Margo and would never be able to understand what I've just told you. And Father avoids all conversations having to do with Mother."
(January 6, 1944)

1 In the autumn of 1942, an additional person comes to hide in the Secret Annex. Otto Frank plays a decisive role in the choice of who, as Anne writes: *"We always thought there was enough room and food for one more person. We were just afraid of placing an even greater burden on Mr. Kugler and Mr. Kleiman. But since reports of the dreadful things being done to the Jews are getting worse by the day, Father sounded out the two people who had to decide, and they thought it was an excellent plan. It wasn't difficult to round someone up. After Father had rejected all the Van Pels' relatives, we chose a dentist named Fritz Pfeffer."* (November 10, 1942)

2 Anne Frank admires her father and is simply crazy about him. She gives him the pet name Pim. *"I love them, but only because they're Mother and Margot, as people they can go fly a kite. It's different with Father.*

When I see him being partial to Margot, approving Margot's every action, praising and hugging her, I feel a gnawing ache inside, because I'm crazy about him. He's the only one I look up to, in the entire world I don' love anyone but Father." (November 7, 1942)

Later Anne's opinion of her father shifts and she distances herself much more. *"I didn't want to hear about 'typical adolescent problems', or 'other girls', or 'you'll grow out of it'. I didn't want to be treated the same as all-the-other-girls, but as Anne-in-her-own-right, and Pim didn't understand that. Besides, I can't confide in anyone unless they tell me a lot about themselves, and because I know very little about Pim, I can't get on a more intimate footing with him. I have concealed everything that bothered me from Father, never shared my ideals with him, and deliberately pushed him away from me."* (July 15, 1944)

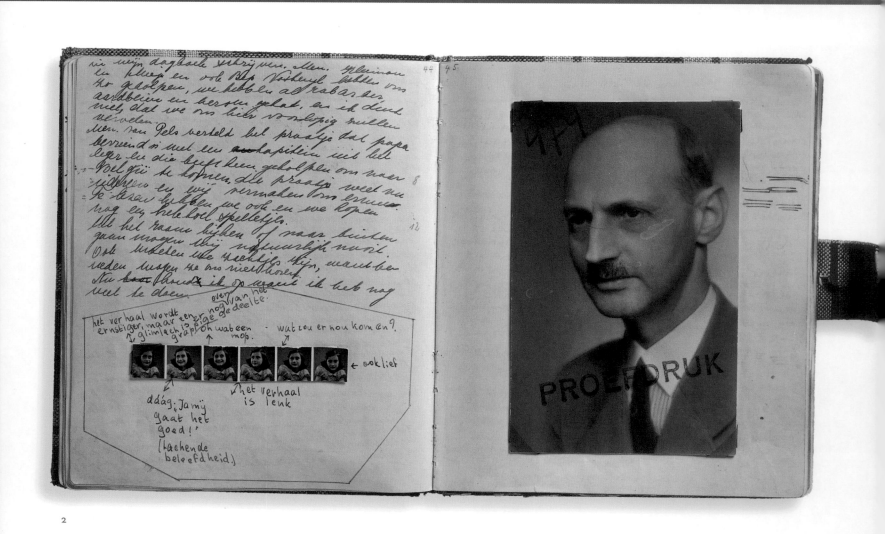

On June 6, 1944, the Allied Forces land in Normandy. Otto Frank keeps track of the progress of the Allied invasion on a small map he's cut out of the daily newspaper *De Telegraaf* (The Telegraph). Every day the people in hiding follow the advance of the Allied Forces on the radio. Anne writes: *"'This is D-day,' the English radio said at twelve o'clock and rightly so! 'This is the day,' came the announcement over the English news at twelve o'clock. The invasion has begun! This morning at eight o'clock the English reported: heavy bombing of Calais, Boulogne, Le Havre, and Cherbourg as well as Pas de Calais. According to German reports English parachute troops have landed on the French Coast. British landing crafts are engaged in combat with the German Marines,' according to the BBC."* (June 6, 1944)

Great commotion in the Annex! Is this really the beginning of the long-awaited liberation? The liber- ation about which so much has been said, but which *seems too wonderful, too much like a fairy tale, ever to come true? Will this year, 1944, bring us victory? We don't know yet, but where there's hope, there's life, and this restores our courage and makes us strong again. Margot says that maybe I can even go back to school in October or September."* (June 6, 1944)

→ You have to walk through the room that Otto, Edith and Margot share to get to the small room of Anne and Fritz Pfeffer. Otto's map of Normandy can be seen hanging on the wall (top right).

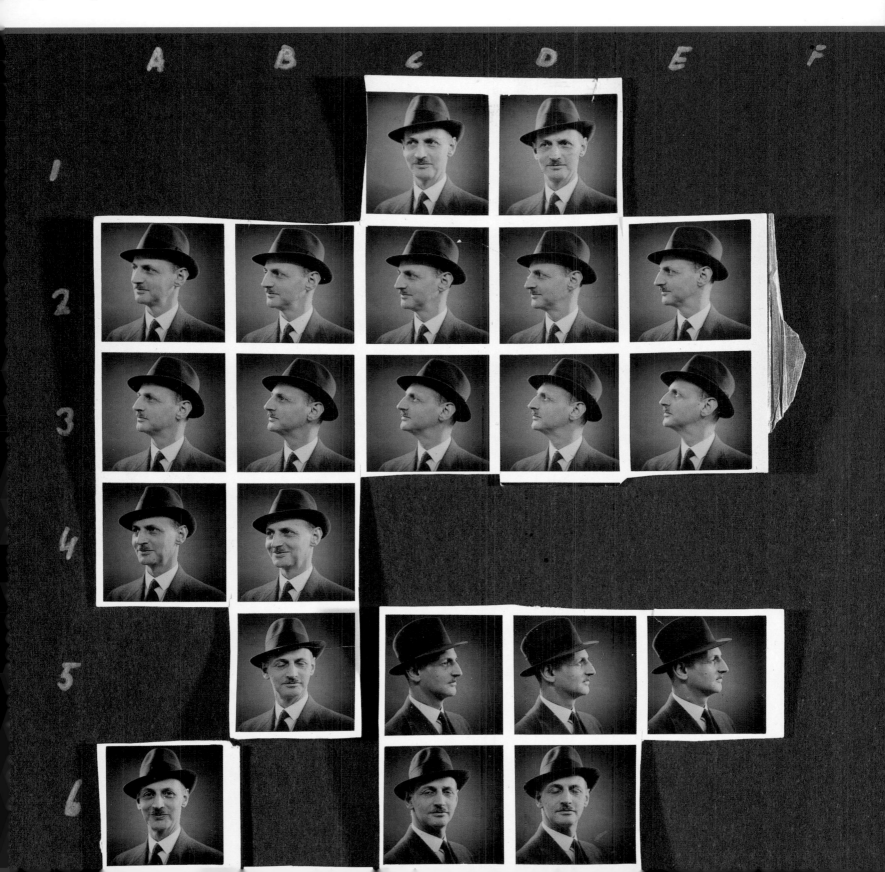

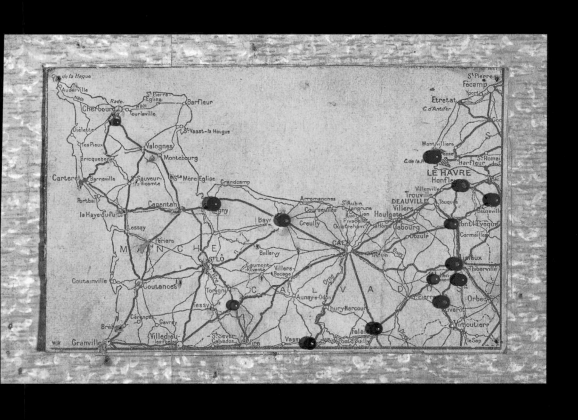

"A smaller room, the bedroom and study of the two young ladies of the Frank family."

July 9, 1942

Anne Frank and Fritz Pfeffer's Room

Anne and Margot sleep together in this room for a number of months. Fritz Pfeffer, the new person in hiding, moves in with Anne in November 1942 and then Margot goes to her parents' room. Anne is initially positive about her new roommate, but that quickly changes and she writes about him in a very negative manner. Both of them prefer to be alone in the small room when writing.

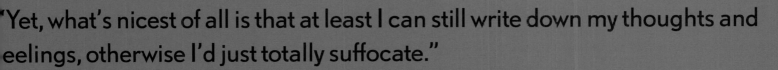

"Yet, what's nicest of all is that at least I can still write down my thoughts and feelings, otherwise I'd just totally suffocate."

March 15, 1944

eading, or working. This causes a great deal of strife. Only once she's lying in

bed at night does Anne have the peace and quiet to think about herself, the others,

the dangers of the outside world, and about day-to-day occurrences. Hope and

fear, low-spirits, the desire to live, falling in love, cheerfulness; Anne writes about

all these emotions in her diary.

1 Essentially the Secret Annex is well concealed from the outside world. In the evenings blackout panels are placed in front of the windows. During the day the windows are covered with curtains. *"Sometimes one of the ladies or gentlemen gets an irresistible urge to peek outside. Result: a storm of criticism. Response: 'Oh, nobody will notice.' That's how every act of negligence begins and ends. Nobody will notice, nobody will hear, no one is interested."* (November 3, 1943)

"We started making curtains right away on the first day, though you can hardly call them that because they're nothing but a few loose pieces of dreary fabric, varying greatly in shape, quality and design, which Father and I crookedly sewed together in a most unprofessional way. These show pieces are tacked in front of the windows, not to be removed until we come out of hiding." (July 11, 1942)

2 Anne's room is just as small as the other rooms. Everyone getting ready for bed in the evenings around 9 o'clock causes quite a commotion: *"Chairs are shoved about, beds pulled out, blankets arranged and nothing stays where it supposedly belongs during the day. I sleep on the small divan which isn't even five feet long. So a few chairs have to be used as extensions."* (August 4, 1943)

Anne glues prints from her collection to the two blank walls of her small room. These images give us an impression of her broad range of interests, for example: film stars, nature, history and royalty. Leonardo da Vinci and Rembrandt alongside Greta Garbo and Ginger Rogers.

"Our little room looked very bare at first with nothing on the walls; but thanks to Daddy who had brought my film-star collection on beforehand, and with the aid of a paste pot and brush, I have transformed the walls into one gigantic picture. This makes it look much more cheerful." (July 11, 1942)

3 Anne misses her girlfriends, school, her cat Mouschi, and is very aware of the constant danger. Jews who have gone into hiding are threatened with severe punishments. *"Not being able to go outside upsets me more than I can say, and I'm terrified that we will be discovered and that we'll be shot."* (September 28, 1942)

1

2

"I spend many Sundays sorting through my large collection of film stars, which has reached quite a respectable size by now." (January 28, 1944)

1 The seventeen-year-old Deanna Durbin (middle) flanked by Robert Stack, acting in a double-role, in the film *First Love*.

2 The actress and figure-skater Sonja Henie with actor Rudy Vallee.

3 The actress Norma Shearer.

4 Heinz Rühmann. A still from the German movie *Paradies der Junggesellen*.

5 Greta Garbo in the film *Ninotchka*, 1939.

6 The screen actor and "lady-killer" Ray Milland.

7 Ginger Rogers.

8 As a thirteen-year-old dancer, Joyce van der Veen is featured in the October 3, 1941 issue of *Libelle*, a popular women's magazine. Anne cuts out her picture and glues it to the wall. Joyce van der Veen is also Jewish and goes into hiding during the war, together with her parents. After the war she emigrates to the United States where she becomes an actress. More than fifty years later, while visiting the Anne Frank House, she sees her photo hanging on the wall. Joyce van der Veen: *"I think that to Anne that picture represented the outside world."*

9 Anne often fantasizes about being an actress in the United States. She also writes a short story about

1

2

3

7

8

9

his entitled: "Dreams of Movie Stardom", in response
o "the questions of Mrs. van Pels who never tires
of asking me why I wouldn't want to become a movie
tar." In the story Anne imagines herself as a seven-
een-year-old girl who ends up in Hollywood as the
uest of a famous film star. But it's not at all what
he expects and she writes: "As for dreams of movie
tardom, I was cured."
Anne's Storybook, December 24, 1943)

Bep, who on her days off often goes to the movies
vith her boyfriend, tells me the titles of the new films
ach Saturday; and in one breath I rattle off the names
f the leading actors as well as what the reviews say.
Moms recently remarked that I wouldn't need to go to
he movies later on because I already know the plots,
he names of the stars and the reviews by heart."
anuary 28, 1944)

10 "This is a photograph of me as I wish I looked all the
time. Then I might still have a chance of getting to
Hollywood. But at present, I'm afraid I usually look
quite different." (October 18, 1942)

4

5

6

Pas op, kleine, met je hoedje!
Tijgers zijn gevaarlijk goedje!

H.R.H. THE PRINCESS ELIZABETH OF YORK

TROUW

H.R.H. THE PRINCESS MARGARET ROSE OF Y...

THE LARK'S SONG
by
Margaret W. Tarrant

NORMA SHEARER

1 Fritz Pfeffer is Miep Gies' dentist and also knows the Frank family well. He asks Miep if she knows of a place to hide. The inhabitants of the Secret Annex agree to his joining them. Anne is even enthusiastic: *"Great news! We're planning to take an eighth person into hiding with us!"* (November 10, 1942) Pfeffer is very surprised to see the Frank Family again on November 16, 1942, because he thought they had left for Switzerland. Anne now shares her small room with Pfeffer.

"Just as we thought, Pfeffer is a very nice man. Of course he didn't mind sharing a room with me; to be honest, I'm not exactly delighted at having a stranger use my things, but you have to make sacrifices for a good cause." (November 19, 1942)

2 Charlotte Kaletta and Fritz Pfeffer around 1940.

1

2

3

Fritz Pfeffer writes, in a farewell letter to Charlotte Kaletta, on November 15, 1942: *"My dearly beloved wife, what can this, hopefully short separation possibly mean compared to our eternal bond? Hold onto your magnificent courage and your trust in God, and your love will make me and us strong and courageous".* In the months that follow, Pfeffer writes letters to her on a regular basis. Miep Gies acts as *postillion d'amour* ('courier of love'), but his place of hiding remains a secret.

Anne's opinion of Pfeffer quickly changes. She is amazed at how slowly he grasps things. *"He asks everything twice and still can't remember anything."* (November 19, 1942)

Fritz Pfeffer brings some of his dental equipment along with him. *"Pfeffer has received a pedal-operated*

dentist's drill. That probably means I'll be getting a thoroughly awful check-up soon."* (March 19, 1943) On one occasion he treats Mrs. van Pels and Anne vividly describes the treatment with much humor. Though at a certain moment she becomes a victim herself. *"I've been having really ghastly root-canal work done on one of my front teeth. It's been terribly painful. It was so bad, Pfeffer thought I was going to faint, and I nearly did. On the spot, Madam (Mrs. van Pels) also felt the pain!"* (June 30, 1944)

"Mr. Pfeffer has turned out to be an old-fashioned disciplinarian and preacher of unbearably long sermons on manners. Since I have the unusual good fortune (!) of being able to share my far too narrow room with His Excellency, and since I'm generally considered to be the most badly brought-up of the three young people, I have my hands quite full – with

tolerating the same old stances and warnings that are repeatedly thrown at my head and with pretending not to hear."* (November 28, 1942)

5 In her diary Anne makes a short list of the activities of the people in hiding. She says concerning Fritz Pfeffer: *"Learns English, Spanish, and Dutch, without noticeable results. Reads everything, agrees with the majority."* (May 16, 1944) Fritz Pfeffer is studying Spanish because he plans to emigrate to South America with Charlotte Kaletta after the war. In his Spanish textbook *Actividades Commerciales* ('Commercial Activities') he makes this notation: "25.VII. 1¹/₂ de la tarde achterhuis". (July 25th, 1:30 in the afternoon, annex)

5

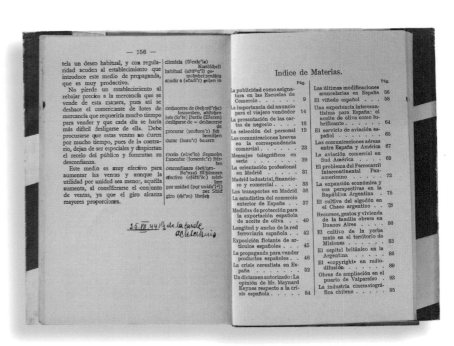

4

5

1 Anne has a great many hobbies and interests. She elaborates on these in her diary entry of April 6, 1944: *"First of all: writing, but I don't really think of that as a hobby."* She further lists tracking down family trees of royal families. *"So my third hobby is history, and Father's already bought me numerous books."* She also mentions collecting photos of moviestars, family photos and art reproductions. The walls of her small room reflect all of these hobbies.

2 The Duke of Reichstadt, Napoleon's son.

3 Self-portrait of Leonardo da Vinci.

4 Detail of Michelangelo's *Pietà*.

5 Rembrandt: *Portrait of an Old Man.*

"By tomorrow I must finish reading the first part of Galileo Galilei. Besides that, I finished reading the first part of a biography about Emperor Charles V yesterday and it's essential that I work out all the notes and genealogical chart I've taken from it. After that I have three pages of foreign words gathered from various books, which have all got to be recited, written down, and memorized." (May 11, 1944)

6 A picture postcard showing members of the Dutch Royal family, who lived in exile in Canada during the war. In the Netherlands the postcard is distributed by the illegal Resistance newspaper *Trouw* ('Loyalty'). *"Bep has had a picture postcard of the entire Royal Family made for me. Juliana looks very young, and so does the Queen. The three little girls are adorable. It was incredibly nice of Bep, don't you think?"* (December 30, 1943)

2

3

1

7

nne keeps a special notebook for copying down quotes and gems of wisdom ("favorite quotes") from e books she reads. The last two "gems" written in er notebook are: *"Deep down the young are lonelier an the old."* and *"One who cannot listen, should ot speak."* (July 2, 1944) When Anne feels the need have a good conversation with Peter, she writes: *might take my 'favorite quotes notebook' up with e sometime so Peter and I can go more deeply into atters for once."* (April 18, 1944)

ight from the very beginning of the hiding period, argot, Anne and Peter keep up with their schoolwork. hey are hopeful that the war will quickly come to an nd and they don't want to have fallen behind in school. tto Frank makes sure that they do their lessons orrectly and helps them when necessary. On April 6, 44 Anne complains: *"I loathe algebra, geometry,*

and arithmetic. I enjoy all my other school subjects, but history's my favorite."

"I must do my schoolwork to keep from being ignorant, to get on with life, to become a journalist, because that's what I want." (April 5, 1944)

4

5

6

8

[A]nne prefers to work at her small desk when writing, [re]ading and studying. But Pfeffer also puts claims on [th]e small table. Anne asks him *"whether he would [p]lease be so good as to allow me (see how polite I am?) [to] use the table in our room two afternoons a week, [fr]om four to five-thirty. I already sit there every day [fr]om two-thirty to four when Pfeffer takes a nap, but [th]e rest of the time the room and the table are off-limits [to] me."* Yet, Pfeffer refuses by saying that anyway Anne [is] not seriously busy. Anne is enraged: *"I let Pfeffer [fi]nish speaking: 'So I see, it's impossible to talk to you. [Yo]u're shamefully self-centered. No one else matters [as] long as you get your way. I've never seen such a [ch]ild.' It just continued along these lines, until finally [th]ere was such a deluge that I could hardly keep track. [At] long last Mr. Pfeffer's fury was spent, and he left the [ro]om with an expression of triumph mixed with wrath."* [Ju]ly 13, 1943)

2 Anne runs to her father, who also ends up having a discussion with Fritz Pfeffer. *"And so the conversation went back and forth, with Father defending my 'selfishness' and my 'busywork' and Pfeffer grumbling the whole time. Pfeffer finally had to give in and I was granted the opportunity to work without interruption two afternoons a week. Pfeffer looked very sullen, didn't speak to me for two days and made sure he occupied the table from five to five-thirty – all very childish, of course. A person of fifty-four who is still so pedantic and small-minded must be so by nature, and will never improve."* (July 13 1943)

[Facsimile of handwritten diary pages in Dutch.]

Left page (6):

genegeerd. Al gauw kon ik dit niet langer uithou-
den en schreef een lange smeekbrief aan klasse 1L_II
om maar weer goed te worden. Nog twee weken later
was het geval vergeten.
De brief was ongeveer als volgt.
Aan de leerlingen van klasse 1L_II.
Hierbij bieden Anne Frank en Lies Goslar hun welgemeen-
de verontschuldiging aan bij de leerling en van klasse
1L_II wegens het laffe verraden van het Franse proef-
werk.
De daad was echter gebeurd voor wij er goed over nage-
dacht hadden en wij geven alle twee volgaarne toe
dat wij eigenlijk alleen de straf hadden moeten dragen.
Wij denken dat het iedereen wel eens zou kunnen
gebeuren dat hij zich een woord of zin in woede
laat ontglippen, die een onaangenaam gevolg heeft,
en toch helemaal niet zo bedoeld was. Wij hopen dat
1L_II het gebeurde ook zo zou willen opvatten en
goed met kwaad vergelden. Het helpt nu ook niet
meer en de twee schuldigen kunnen de daad niet
meer ongedaan maken.
Wij zouden deze brief niet schrijven als wij niet
werkelijk spijt van het gebeurde hadden. Verder
vragen wij nog aan degenen die ons tot heden ne-
geerden, daarmede op te willen houden, want zo
groot was de daad toch niet om tot in de eeuwig-
heid als een misdadiger te worden aangezien.
Laat wie nu nog niet over ons of onze daad weg
kan stappen, naar ons toe komen en ons een flinke
uitbrander geven of op de een of andere manier
een dienst vragen, wij zullen deze als het ons enigs-
zins mogelijk is zeker inwilligen.
Wij vertrouwen dat nu alle leerlingen van klasse 1L_II
het gebeurde zullen vergeten.
Anne Frank en
Lies Goslar.

Weet je nog? Hoe Puri Pimentel in de klas tegen
Rob Cohen zei. Zodat Sanne Ledermann, het
hoorde en het mij toen later vertelde, dat Anne
toch veel knapper van gezicht was, dan Sanne
zeide, vooral als ze lachte. Het antwoord
van Rob was: Wat heb jij toch een grote neusgaten,

Right page (7):

Puri!"

Weet je nog? Hoe Maurice Coster zich bij Puri wou aan-
melden om ingang met z'n dochter te vragen.

Weet je nog? Hoe Rob Cohen en Anne Frank een drukke
briefwisseling hadden, tijdens dat Rob in het ziekenhuis
lag.

Weet je nog? Hoe Sam Salomon me altijd aldoor achterna reed
op de fiets en me een arm wilde geven.

Weet je nog? Hoe Bram Rocker me een zoen op m'n wang
gaf, bij de klofte dat ik niets aan wie ook zou vertellen
van Lies Held en hem zelf.

Ik hoop dat er ooit nog eens zo'n onbezorgde schooltijd
terug zal komen.

Het laatste Tafeltje.
Vrijdag 13 Juli '43
Gisteren middag heb ik met beiden verlof aan Pf.
gevraagd of hij het als 't u blieft goed zou willen
vinden, (toch zeg beleefd) dat ik 2x in de week van
ons tafeltje 's middags van 4 - 5½ uur gebruik zou
kunnen maken. Van 2½ - 4 uur zit ik daar al elke
dag, terwijl Pf. slaapt en verder is de kamer + tafeltje
verboden terrein. Binnen is onze algemene kamer
is het 's middags veel te druk daar kan men niet
werken, en trouwens onder zit 's middags toch ook
wel eens graag te werken aan de schrijftafel.
De reden was dus redelijk en de vraag alleen zuivere be-
leefdheid. Wat denk je nu wel, dat die hooggeleerde Pf.
antwoordde: "nee!" Betweg en alleen maar "nee!"
Ik was verontwaardigd en liet me niet zomaar afschepen,
vroeg hem dus de reden van zijn "nee". Maar ik kwam
van een koude kermis thuis. Hierdaar de lading die
volgde:
"Ik moet ook werken, als ik niet 's middags kan werken schiet er voor mij helemaal geen tijd meer over
ik moet m'n pensum afkrijgen, anders ben ik
er voor niets aan begonnen. Gij werkt toch niet eenvoudig
die mythologie, wat is dat nou voor werk, breien en lezen
is ook geen werk, ik ben en blijf aan dat tafeltje!"

When she's lying in bed in the evenings and in the middle of the night, Anne has the time and space to think about herself and others.

"Oh well, so much comes into my head at night when I'm alone, or during the day when I'm obliged to put up with people I can't abide or who invariably misinterpret my intentions. That's why I always wind up coming back to my diary – I start there and end there because Kitty's always patient. I promise her that, despite everything, I'll keep on going. I'll pave my own way and I'll swallow my tears."

November 7, 1942

Anne frequently wakes-up in the middle of the night and then she listens to the nightly sounds
"In the first place, to hear if there are any burglars downstairs, and then to the various beds – upstairs, next door and in my room – to tell whether the others are asleep or half awake. This is no fun, especially when it concerns a member of the family named Dr. Pfeffer. First there's the sound of a fish gasping for air, and this is repeated nine or ten times. Then the lips are moistened profusely. This is alternated with little smacking sounds, followe by a long period of tossing and turning and rearranging the pillows. "

August 4, 1943

Sometimes Anne despairs:
"At night in bed I see myself alone in a dungeon, without Father and Mother. Or I'm roaming the streets, or the Annex is on fire, or they come in the middle of the night to take us away and I crawl under my bed in desperation. I see everything as if it were actually taking place. And to think it might all happen soon! I simply can't imagine the world will ever be normal again for us."

November 8, 1943

nne desperately yearns for the open air.

Whenever someone comes in from outside, with the wind in their clothes and the cold
n their cheeks, I feel like burying my head under the blankets to keep from thinking:
Vhen will we be allowed to breathe fresh air again?' And because I'm not allowed to do
at – on the contrary, I have to hold my head up high and put a bold face on things, but the
oughts keep coming anyway. Not just once, but over and over, countless times. Believe me,
you've been shut up for a year and a half, it sometimes gets to be too much. But feelings
an't be ignored, no matter how unjust or ungrateful they seem. I long to ride a bike, dance,
histle, look at the world, feel young and know that I'm free."

ecember 24, 1943

1. Tuesday, March 28, 1944 is an important day for Anne. *"Mr. Bolkestein, the Cabinet Minister, speaking on the Dutch broadcast from London, said that after the war, a collection would be made of diaries and letters dealing with the war. Of course everyone pounced on my diary. Just imagine how interesting it would be if I were to publish a novel about the Secret Annex. The title alone would make people think it was a detective story."* (March 29, 1944) Anne decides to edit her diary notes so she can publish them later on.

"But, and that's a big question, will I ever be able to write something great, will I ever become a journalist or a writer? I hope so, oh I hope so very much, because writing allows me to record everything, all my thoughts, ideals and fantasies." (April 5, 1944)

2. Sometimes Anne has serious doubts about her end result. *"My writing's all mixed up, I'm jumping from one thing to another and sometimes I seriously doubt whether anyone will ever be interested in this drivel. They'll probably call it 'The Musings of an Ugly Duckling'".* (April 14, 1944)

3. Anne doesn't only write in her diary. In a large, hardcover notebook she also jots down "Stories and events from the Secret Annex". She describes a praying Fritz Pfeffer as follows: *"One of my Sunday morning ordeals is having to lie in bed and look at Pfeffer's back when he's praying. I know it sounds strange, but a praying Pfeffer is a terrible sight to behold. It's not that he cries or gets sentimental, not at all, but he does spend a quarter of an hour – an entire fifteen minutes – rocking from his toes to his heels.*

Back and forth, back and forth. It goes on forever, and if I don't shut my eyes tight, my head starts to spin. (February 20, 1944)

Still, the diary remains Anne's most important project. She has ambitions: *"I know I can write. A few of my stories are good, my descriptions of the Secret Annex are humorous, much of my diary is vivid and alive, but...it remains to be seen whether I really have talent. I want to achieve more. I can't imagine having to live like Mother, Mrs. van Pels and all the women who go about their work and are then forgotten."* (April 5, 1944)

"I don't want to have lived in vain like most people. I want to be useful or bring enjoyment to all people, even those I've never met. I want to go on living even

1

2

"...fter my death! And therefore I am so grateful to God
...or giving me this gift, this possibility of developing
...myself and of writing, of expressing all that is in me!"
...April 5, 1944)

"A windowless room, containing the washbasin and small w.c. compartment, with another door leading to Margot's and my room."

July 9, 1942

The Bathroom

Eight people having access to only one toilet and sink means that those in hiding often have to wait their turn. The additional problem exists that the facilities cannot be used too often, because the sound of streaming water could give them away. For instance, the toilet may be flushed in the daytime during office hours,

"Margot and Mother are nervous. 'Shh... Father, be quiet, Otto, ssh...Come here, you can't run the water any more. Walk softly!' A sample of what's said to Father in the bathroom."

Anne's Storybook, August 6, 1943

but not too frequently. It can definitely be heard in the warehouse, but the

workers there do not suspect that anyone else other than the office employees

could be responsible for the sound. The toilet is also a place for the people in

hiding to retreat to, to find some privacy in the crowded Secret Annex.

1 Fritz Pfeffer often goes to the toilet so he can be alone for a moment. Anne characterizes him as follows: *"Pants that come up to his chest, a red jacket, black patent-leather slippers and horn-rimmed glasses – that's how he looks when he's at work at the little table, always studying and never progressing. This is interrupted only by his afternoon nap, food and – his favorite spot – the bathroom. Three, four or five times a day there's bound to be someone waiting outside the bathroom door, hopping impatiently from one foot to another, trying to hold it in and barely managing. Does Pfeffer care? Not a whit."* (August 9, 1943) Yet, Anne often has the need to be alone for just a moment too.

"Suddenly I felt the tears coming again. I raced downstairs to the bathroom, grabbing the hand mirror on the way. I sat there on the toilet, fully dressed, *long after I was through, my tears leaving dark spots on the red of my apron, and I felt utterly wretched."* (February 19, 1944)

2 Anne continues to be annoyed with the toilet behavior of Pfeffer. *"This afternoon I boldly took a piece of pink paper and wrote:*
Mr. Pfeffer's Toilet Timetable
Mornings from 7:15 - 7:30 A.M.
Afternoons after 1:00 P.M.
Otherwise, only as needed!
I tacked this to the green bathroom door while he was still inside. I might well have added: Transgressors will be subject to confinement! Because our bathroom can be locked from both the inside and the outside."
(May 9, 1944)

1

2

3

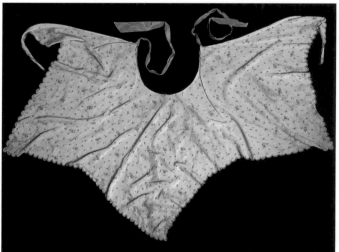

4

The people in hiding are not allowed to regularly flush the toilet, because that could give them away. Even Peter, though he's usually quiet, occasionally gives rise to hilarity. One afternoon we couldn't use the toilet because there were visitors in the office. Unable to wait, he went to the bathroom, but didn't flush the toilet. To warn us of the unpleasant odor, he tacked a sign to the bathroom door: 'SVP-gas!' Of course he meant 'Danger – gas!,' but he thought 'SVP'* looked more elegant." (February 5, 1943)
(* French: s'il vous plaît or 'if you please')

Anne's hairdressing cape. Anne pays a lot of attention to her appearance. Especially to her hair. Anne goes into the bathroom every evening around nine o'clock, and spends a good half-hour there.

5   "After Peter's finished, it's my turn for the bathroom. I wash myself from head to toe, and more often than not I find a tiny flea floating in the sink (only during the hot months, weeks or days). I brush my teeth, curl my hair, manicure my nails and dab peroxide on my upper lip to bleach the black hairs – all this in less than half an hour. Nine-thirty: I throw on my bathrobe. With soap in one hand, and potty, hairpins, panties, curlers and a wad of cotton in the other, I hurry out of the bathroom. The next in line invariably calls me back to remove the unsightly hairs which I've left in the sink."
(August 4, 1943)

"If you go up the stairs and open the door at the top, you're surprised to see such a large, light and spacious room in an old canalside house like this. It contains a stove (thanks to the fact that it used to be Mr. Kugler's laboratory) and a sink. This will be the kitchen and bedroom of Mr. and Mrs. van Pels, as well as the general living room, dining room and study for us all."

July 9, 1942

Hermann and Auguste van Pels' Room

On the top floor of the Secret Annex is Hermann and Auguste van Pels' room, which at the same time functions as the common living room. Around noontime, the helpers from the office and Jan Gies come to eat lunch here. In the evening all eight people in hiding and the helper Bep Voskuijl eat at the large table in this room. Now and then, Mr. and Mrs. Kleiman visit on the weekend.

"Nine o'clock, Sunday evening. The teapot, under its cozy, is on the table, and the guests enter the room. Pfeffer sits to the left of the radio, Mr. v.P. in front of it and Peter to the side. Mother is next to Mr. v.P., with Mrs. v.P. behind them. Margot and I are sitting in the last row and Pim at the table."

March 27, 1944

Mr. and Mrs. van Pels therefore have even less privacy than the Frank family. The joint meals offer companionship, but also give rise to conflicts, for instance, about upbringing. "To not fancy some kind of food" is inconceivable for the van Pelses, while Anne finds this very normal. As time passes being in hiding becomes more difficult. Not only do supplies shrink, tensions also increase.

Upon their arrival at the Secret Annex on July 13, 1942, 'Mr. v.P.' and 'Mrs. v.P.' (or Madam) – as Anne usually refers to the Van Pelses – bring along a few unusual personal objects. *"Mrs. v.P. was carrying a hatbox with a large potty inside. 'I just don't feel at home without my chamber pot,' she exclaimed, and it was the first item to find a permanent place under the divan. Instead of a chamber pot, Mr. v.P. was lugging a collapsible tea table under his arm. From the first, we ate our meals together, and after three days it felt as if the seven of us had become one big family."* (August 14, 1942)

1 In this room, all the people in hiding gather for preparing and eating meals and at anxious moments. Even though everyone takes part in the housekeeping chores, this sometimes still leads to quarreling. One of Anne's "short stories" is devoted to this: "The Battle of

e Potatoes" (August 4, 1943). According to Hermann
n Pels, Anne and Margot would *"be better off, if they
elped out more instead of always having their noses
 a book, it isn't necessary for girls to learn so much!"*
dith Frank does not agree with this at all and *"there-
re it doesn't happen".*

After about three months of peace, interrupted
y occasional bickering, there was a big fight today.
Mrs. v.P. started it (as usual) by saying that anyone
ho didn't help with the potato peeling in the morning
ould have to help in the evening. Nobody answered,
nd that didn't suit the Van Pelses at all because a
inute later Mr. v.P. said the best way would be for
veryone to peel his own potatoes, except Peter,
ecause potato peeling wasn't suitable work for boys.
You see his brand of logic!)."* (Anne's Storybook,
ugust 4, 1943)

2 *"The seven of us had seated ourselves around the
dining table to await the latest addition to our family
with coffee and cognac,"* so Anne relates in her diary
on November 17, 1942, about the arrival of Fritz Pfeffer,
the eighth person in hiding. Especially for Pfeffer,
Hermann van Pels puts down the Secret Annex's rules
of hiding on paper, entitled: *"Prospectus and Guide to
the Secret Annex: A Unique Facility for the Temporary
Accommodation of Jews and the Like."* Anne Frank
copies these typed house rules into her diary.

3 The *Prospectus* of Hermann van Pels is an ironic
description of the Secret Annex. *"Open all year round.
Located in beautiful, quiet, wooded surroundings in
the heart of Amsterdam. No private residencies in the
vicinity. Can be reached by streetcar 13 and 17 and also
by car and bicycle. For those to whom such transportation has been forbidden by the German authorities,*
*it can also be reached on foot. Furnished and unfur-
nished apartments and rooms are available at all
times, with or without meals. Price: Free. Diet: Low-fat.
Running water in the bathroom (sorry no bath) and
on various inside and outside walls. Private radio with
a direct line to London, New York, Tel Aviv and many
other stations."*

*"Some people, seem to take special delight in raising
not only their own children but in helping others raise
theirs, for instance v.P.'s. You should hear us at
mealtimes, with reprimands and saucy replies flying
to and fro. If I take a small helping of some vegetable
I detest and eat potatoes instead, the v.P.'s, and
Madam in particular, can't get over how spoiled I am.
'Come on, Anne, eat some more vegetables,' she says."*
(September 27, 1942)

2

1 Hermann van Pels loves good food, likes to crack a joke and is usually in a bad mood when there's a shortage of cigarettes. He has an outspoken opinion about politics and willingly speculates about the duration of the war. In contrast to the other Secret Annex occupants, he does not follow any study courses. He enjoys looking things up in the encyclopedia and reads preferably *"detective stories, medical books and love stories, exciting and trivial,"* as Anne describes it. While in hiding he works for Otto's business. In the evening he regularly goes to the warehouse where the spice mixtures are made. (May 16, 1944)

"Usually joins in the conversation, never fails to give his opinion. Once he's spoken, his word is final. If anyone dares to suggest otherwise, he can put up a good fight. Oh...he can hiss like a cat... but I'd rather he didn't... Once you've seen it, you never want to see it again.

His opinion is the best, he knows the most about everything. Granted, the man has a good head on his shoulders, but it's swelled to no small degree." (August 9, 1943)

2 Hermann van Pels makes this shopping list for Miep Gies. *"To Credit: Three coupons,"* so it says, *"two for the liver-sausage and one for the blood-sausage."* The list for the order continues: *"One and a half blood-sausage, one blood-sausage and one and a half liver-sausage. Calf legs or a small calf's head."* Hermann van Pels has many contacts in the butcher's branch who deliver extra meat without ration coupons. As early as the spring of 1942, he takes Miep Gies along with him to a sympathetic butcher in the neighborhood. At first Miep does not understand why. Later, this butcher helps Miep when she comes to do the shopping for the people in hiding.

"Mr. van Pels used to be in the meat, sausage, and spice business. We ordered a large amount of meat (under the counter, of course) which we were planning to preserve in case there were hard times ahead. He proposed making frying sausages, Gelderland sausages and sausage spread. It was such a comical sight. The room was in a glorious mess: Mr. v.P., clad in his wife's apron and looking fatter than ever, was working away at the meat. What with his bloody hands, red face and spotted apron, he looked like a real butcher." (December 10, 1942)

3 *"Today is Mr. van Pels' birthday. He received two packets of tobacco, one serving of coffee, which his wife had managed to save, lemon punch from Mr. Kugler, sardines from Miep, eau de cologne from us, lilacs, tulips and, last but not least, a cake with raspberry filling, slightly gluey because of the poor*

3

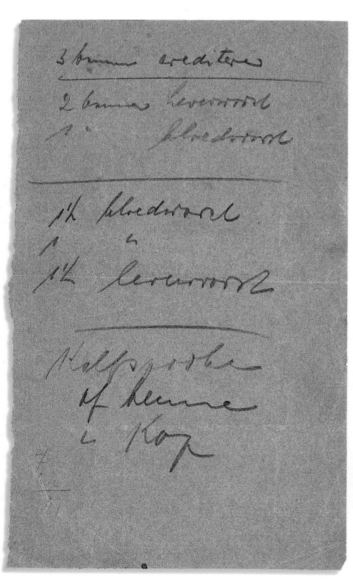

2

1

uality of the flour and the lack of butter, but delicious nyway." (March 31, 1944)

Mr. van Pels: In the opinion of us all, this revered entleman has great insight into politics. Nevertheless, e predicts we'll have to stay here until the end of '43. hat's a very long time, and yet it's possible to hold out ntil then. But who can assure us that this war, which as caused nothing but pain and sorrow, will then be ver? And that nothing will have happened to us nd our helpers long before that time? No one! hat's why each and every day is filled with tension." May 2, 1943)

there is an imminent danger, this room is the fur- est away from the entrance and therefore the safest. there happen to be people in the house who are not ware of the situation, such as the cleaning lady and the

carpenter or even burglars, the people in hiding gather nervously together in this room and remain as quiet as possible. Once the door is closed, few sounds penetrate.

1 While in hiding, Auguste van Pels, or Gusti, attempts to learn Dutch. *"Mrs. van Pels. was trying to do everything at once: learning Dutch out of a book, stirring the soup, watching the meat, sighing and moaning about her broken rib."* (December 10, 1942) Anne comments a lot about the Dutch of "Madam", as well as that of her mother. *"That irritated Mrs. v.P., who continued her story with a string of splendid German-Dutch, Dutch-German expressions, until the born debater became so completely tongue-tied; that she rose from her chair and wanted to leave the room."* (September 28, 1942)

"Smile coquettishly, pretend you know everything, offer everyone a piece of advice and mother them – that's sure to make a good impression. But if you take a better look, the good impression fades. One, she's hard working; two, cheerful; three, coquettish – and sometimes a cute face. That's Gusti van Pels." (August 9, 1943)

2 Auguste van Pels is the "hard-working housewife" and the chief cook of the Secret Annex. Anne's opinion about "Madam" changes repeatedly, and she can write volumes about her. Sometimes Anne can have a good conversation with her, the next moment she finds her unbearable and pretentious and then once again cheerful, industrious and tidy. Auguste likes to read biographies and novels. She learns English by correspondence course. She occupies herself further with knitting, cooking, doing the wash, and if we are to believe Anne, complaining and causing trouble. She also exercises.

3 Looking outside from the Secret Annex is dangerous. During the day getting a breath of fresh air is also a problem. All these restrictions are not conducive to being in a good mood. *"Mrs. v.P. was in a bad mood this morning. All she did was complain, first about*

2

3

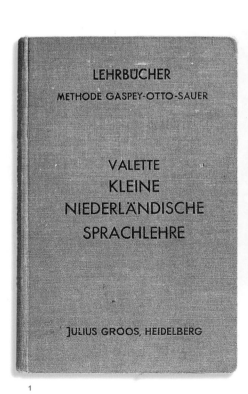

1

er cold, not being able to get cough drops and the
gony of having to blow your nose all the time.
Next she grumbled that the sun wasn't shining, the
nvasion hadn't started, we weren't allowed to look
ut the windows, etc., etc. We couldn't help but laugh
t her, and it couldn't have been that bad, since she
oon joined in." (April 27, 1944)

Mrs. van Pels is unbearable. I'm continually being
colded for my incessant chatter when I'm upstairs.
simply let the words bounce right off me!"
eptember 21, 1942)

'd just finished writing something about Mrs. v.P.
hen she walked into the room. Thump, I slammed
e book shut. 'Hey, Anne, can't I even take a peek?'
No, Mrs. van Pels.' 'Just the last page then?' 'No, not
ven the last page, Mrs. van Pels.' Of course I nearly

died, since that particular page contained a rather
unflattering description of her." (September 21, 1942)

1 Listening to the radio is a regular part of the daily routine. *"Clustered around the radio, they all listen raptly to the BBC. This is the only time the members of the Annex family don't interrupt each other, since even Mr. van Pels can't argue with the speaker."* (August 5, 1943) One of the BBC commentators, Mr. Beaverbrook, thinks the bombings on Germany are not heavy enough. Because Mrs. van Pels agrees with him, but never with her husband, the others call her "Mrs. Beaverbrook".

"A little discussion that went on between Mr. and Mrs. v.P. last night: Mr. v.P.: 'My predictions have come true up till now.' Mrs. v.P.: 'That's not true. You said the invasion was going to start last year, the Finns were supposed to have been out of the war by now, the Italian campaign ought to have been over by last winter and the Russians should already have captured *Lemberg. Oh no, I don't set much store by your predictions.'"* (May 16, 1944)

2 The Van Pelses' room in 1954. Tensions are unavoidable when eight people live so closely together for such a long time. Besides temperamental clashes between various persons, sometimes clear differences of opinion emerge between "upstairs" and "downstairs". For example about how to raise children, what they may and may not read, eat, know. *"Relationships here in the Annex are getting worse all the time. We don't dare open our mouths at mealtime (except to slip in a bite of food), because no matter what we say, someone is bound to resent it or take it the wrong way."* (September 16, 1943)

3 The stove is in the corner next to the sink. The heater not only serves in providing warmth, but is also used to burn the trash. Those in hiding cannot put any garbage

the trash cans, because the warehousemen would notice this. Therefore everything has to be burned, also when temperatures are extremely high. Yet because of the neighbors this is still extra risky. Especially on weekends, when nobody is working at the company, it's suspicious if smoke comes out of the chimney. So the heater is stoked very early on Sunday mornings when the neighbors are still asleep.

My mind boggles at the profanities this honorable house has had to endure in the past month. Father walks around with his lips pressed together, and whenever he hears his name, he looks up in alarm, as if he's afraid he'll be called upon to resolve another delicate problem. Mother's so wrought up, her cheeks are blotched with red, Margot complains of headaches, Pfeffer can't sleep, Mrs. v.P. frets and fumes all day long, and I've gone completely round the bend.

To tell you the truth, I sometimes forget who we're at odds with and who we're not." (October 17, 1943)

To come by food and other necessary goods one needs not only ration coupons but money as well. The people in hiding are eating into their financial reserves. *"The disagreeable fact is that Mr. van Pels has run out of money,"* writes Anne on October 17, 1943. The couple attempts to sell things, but there appears to be no market for Peter's bicycle and Hermann's suits. *"You see, Mrs. v.P. is going to have to part with her fur coat. In her opinion the firm should pay for our upkeep, but that's ridiculous. Upstairs, they just had a flaming argument about it and have entered the 'Oh my sweet Putti' and 'darling Kerli' stage of reconciliation."*

1

3

1 In November of 1942, the people in hiding and the
helpers buy six large bags of dried beans. Just as
Peter is hoisting a bag up to the attic, a seam breaks.
With a thundering noise the brown beans roll downstairs. Anne is standing at the foot of the stairs up to her
ankles in the beans. *"We promptly began picking them
up, but beans are so small and slippery that they roll
into every conceivable corner and hole. Now each time
we go upstairs, we bend over and hunt around so we
can present Mrs. v.P. with a handful of beans."*

2 Scarcely two years later things are not going as well
with the availability of food. Less and less fresh food can
be found in the stores and the prices are on the rise.
*"As of tomorrow, we won't have a scrap of fat, butter or
margarine. Lunch today consists of mashed potatoes
and pickled kale. You wouldn't believe how much kale
can stink when it's a few years old!"* (March 14, 1944)

*"Since the last raging quarrels, things have settled
down here, not only between ourselves, Pfeffer
and 'upstairs', but also between Mr. and Mrs. v.P.
Nevertheless, a few dark thunderclouds are
heading this way, and all because of...food."*
(December 30, 1943)

3 A menu for a dinner in the Secret Annex, on July 18,
1942, in celebration of the one year wedding anniver-
sary of Jan and Miep Gies. With rather limited means
the people in hiding are able to prepare a chic-looking
meal. Those in hiding and the helpers gladly seize every
opportunity to organize something festive. Therefore,
despite a shortage of candles, they still celebrate the
Jewish Chanukah Festival. Hermann van Pels makes
the Menorah (candle holder) himself. There is also
a large celebration organized for the traditional
Dutch St. Nicholas evening, complete with poems

d small gifts. And sometimes the children entertain
eir parents by dressing up in costumes.

n various festive occasions either Auguste or Edith
akes a cake. Sometimes Miep arranges the cake, for
ample on Christmas and New Year's Eve 1943, with
e inscription: "Peace 1944". A cake recipe written
n the back of a shopping list.

*f the talk at mealtime isn't about politics or good
od, then Mother or Mrs. v.P. trot out stories about
eir childhood which we've heard a thousand times
fore, or Pfeffer goes on and on about beautiful race
orses, his wife's extensive wardrobe etcetera."*
nuary 28, 1944)

ver the course of time, the table conversations
come rather predictable: *"Whenever one of the*

*eight of us opens his mouth, the other seven can finish
the story for him. We know the punch line of every
joke before it gets told, so that whoever's telling it is
left to laugh alone. The various milkmen, grocers and
butchers of the two ex-housewives have already grown
beards in our eyes, so often have they been praised
to the skies or pulled to pieces. There's absolutely no
chance of anything new or fresh being brought up for
discussion in the Annex."* (January 28, 1944)

1

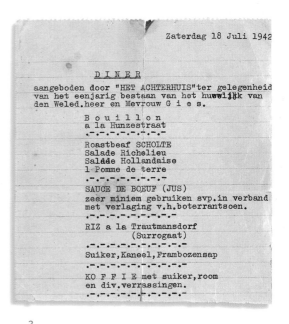

3

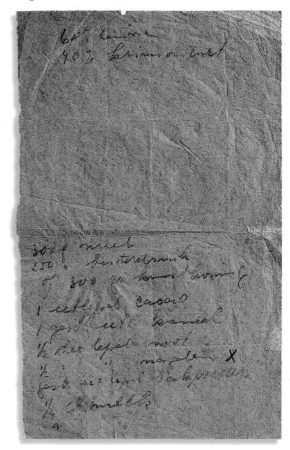

4

There are elaborate discussions held about whether the windows may be opened a small crack at night. At first the windows are opened, but later it's considered to be too dangerous. At night all noises travel much further.

"Upstairs it sounds like thunder, but it's only Mrs. v.P.'s bed being shoved against the window so that Her Majesty, arrayed in her pink bed jacket, can sniff the night air through her delicate little nostrils."

August 4, 1943

"One night Mrs. v.P. thought she heard loud footsteps in the attic, and she was so afraid of burglars, she woke her husband. At that very same moment, the thieves disappeared, and the only sound Mr. v.P. could hear was the frightened pounding of his fatalistic wife's heart."

March 10, 1943

'Oh, Putti!' (Mr. van Pels' pet name) 'They must have taken all our sausages and dried
eans. And what about Peter? Oh, do you think Peter's still safe and sound in his bed?'
'm sure they haven't stolen Peter. Stop being such a ninny, and let me get back to sleep!'
mpossible. Mrs. v.P. was too scared to sleep. A few nights later the entire Van Pels family
as awakened by ghostly noises. Peter went to the attic with a flashlight and – scurry,
curry – what do you think he saw running away? A whole slew of enormous rats!"
March 10, 1943

"If, towards evening, you knock on the door of his room and hear him call a soft 'Come in!' you can be sure that when the door opens, you'll find him looking at you through two of the rungs of the ladder to the attic and saying, 'So!' in a gentle inviting tone. His little room is – what is it really? I think it's a passageway to the attic, very narrow, very dark and damp, but... he has turned it into a real room."

Anne's Storybook, February 22, 1944

Peter van Pels' Room and the Attic

Anne carefully describes Peter van Pels' small room in in her storybook.

In order to practice her writing, she creates an imaginary interview with Peter.

"My First Interview" begins with a detailed description of his room. At first Anne

doesn't think much of Peter, a boring boy. Later on she considerably adjusts

Yesterday was Peter's birthday. At eight o'clock I went upstairs and looked
t the presents with Peter. He received e.g. a board game, a razor, and a lighter."

ovember 9 and 10, 1942

er opinion: she falls in love with him. She receives her first kiss from him.

his infatuation wears off after a little while and Anne looks for ways to distance

erself from Peter. At the moment of the arrest, Otto Frank is giving English

essons to Peter in this room.

1 In the middle of Peter's room is the stairway that goes to the attic of the Secret Annex. This attic is the only place where he and Anne can be alone. In the attic there's a narrow stairway leading to the garret. During the hiding period, food provisions and books are kept in the attic.

"Peter van Pels arrived at nine-thirty in the morning (while we were still at breakfast). Peter's going on sixteen, a shy, awkward boy whose company won't amount to much. Mr. and Mrs. van Pels came half an hour later." (August 14, 1942)

2 On November 8, 1942, Peter turns sixteen-years-old. Anne goes upstairs to take a look at the presents. He receives, among other things, a board game, a razor and a cigarette lighter. *"Not that he smokes so much, not at all, it just looks so distinguished."*

(November 9, 1942) During the Easter holidays of 1944 the people in hiding play the stock-market board game for two afternoons straight.

3 At first Anne doesn't want to have anything to do with Peter. She even complains to his parents about the fact that he often strokes her cheek with his hand. *"They asked me in a typical way parents do whether I couldn't learn to be fond of Peter, since he certainly was fond of me. I thought 'Oh, dear!' and said, 'Oh, no!' Just imagine! Then I said that Peter's a bit stiff, but that it was probably shyness." (September 25, 1942)* Still, Anne's attitude regarding Peter will change dramatically during the course of the hiding period.

"My longing for someone to talk to has become so unbearable that I somehow took it into my head to

2

1

3

lect Peter for this role. On the few occasions when
ave gone to Peter's room during the day, I've always
ought it was nice and cozy. But Peter's too polite to
ow someone the door when they're bothering him,
I've never dared to stay long. I've always been afraid
'd think I was a pest." (January 6, 1944)

ter van Pels' room in 1954.

ne looks for a way to get to know Peter better.
ve been looking for an excuse to linger in his room
d get him talking without his noticing, and yesterday
ot my chance. Peter, you see, is currently going
rough a crossword-puzzle craze. I was helping
m, and we soon wound up sitting across from each
her at his table: Peter on the chair and me on the
van. You mustn't think I'm in love with Peter, because
n not. If the Van Pelses had had a daughter instead

of a son, I'd have tried to make friends with her."
(January 6, 1944)

1 Only in the attic can Anne and Peter spend time together alone. During the working week, Anne comes upstairs to the attic at lunchtime for three-quarters of an hour to get a breath of fresh air. *"The weather is gorgeous, indescribably beautiful; I'll be going up to the attic in a moment. I now know why I'm so much more restless than Peter. He has his own room, where he can work, dream, think and sleep. I'm constantly being chased from one corner to another. I'm never alone in the room I share with Pfeffer, though I long to be so much. That's another reason I take refuge in the attic. When I'm there, or with you, I can be myself, at least for a little while. Still, I don't want to moan and groan. On the contrary, I want to be brave!"* (March 16, 1944)

"I managed to get hold of Peter this afternoon, and we talked for at least forty-five minutes.

He wanted to tell me something about himself, but didn't find it easy. He finally got it out, though it took a long time. I honestly didn't know whether it was better for me to stay or go. But I wanted so much to help him. He told me that his parents fight constantly, about politics and cigarettes and all kinds of things. As I've told you before, Peter's very shy, but not too shy to admit that he'd be perfectly happy not to see his parents for a year or two." (March 2, 1944)

2 *"But...there's someone else who governs all my moods and that's...Peter. Oh, he gazes at me with such warmth in his eyes; I don't think it will take much for me to fall in love with him. In any case, we're getting to know each other a little better. I wish we dared to say more. But who knows, maybe that time will come sooner than I think! Once or twice a day he gives me* →

a knowing glance, I wink back and we're both happy." (March 3, 1944)

3 *"Peter often says 'Smile!' I thought it was strange, so yesterday I asked him: 'Why do you always want me to smile?' 'Because you get dimples in your cheeks. How do you do that?' 'I was born with them. There's also one in my chin. It's the only mark of beauty I possess.' 'No, no, that's not true!' 'Yes it is, I know I'm not beautiful. I never have been and I never will be!' 'I don't agree, I think you're pretty.' 'I am not.' 'I say you are, and you'll have to take my word for it!' So of course I then said the same about him."* (March 28, 1944)

From the attic a narrow stairway leads to the garret. One night Peter goes upstairs to get some old newspapers. *"He had to hold on tightly to the trap door to climb down the ladder. He put down his hand without*

oking, and nearly fell off the ladder from shock
nd pain. Without realizing it, he'd put his hand on a
rge rat, which had bitten him in the arm. By the time
e reached us, white as a sheet and with his knees
nocking, the blood had soaked through his pajamas.
o wonder he was so shaken, since petting a rat isn't
uch fun, especially when it takes a chunk out of your
rm." (March 10, 1943)

ne morning when Anne goes to the attic again,
eter is busy cleaning up. She sits on her favorite spot
n the ground. Peter finishes quickly and joins her.
nne writes: *"The two of us looked out at the blue sky,
e bare chestnut tree glistening with dew, the seagulls
nd other birds glinting with silver as they swooped
rough the air, and we were so moved and entranced
at we couldn't speak. He stood with his head against
thick beam, while I sat."* (February 23, 1944)

1

3

2

1 Anne desperately longs for a kiss from Peter, a kiss that just doesn't come. She wonders if he regards her only as a pal. And if maybe he isn't in love with her after all. *"I've never been used to sharing my worries with anyone, I've never clung to a mother. But I'd love to lay my head on his shoulder and just sit there quietly."* (April 1, 1944)

"Remember yesterday's date, since it was a red-letter day for me. Isn't it an important day for every girl when she gets her first kiss?" (April 16, 1944)

2 One night she is sitting together with Peter on the couch in his room. They are leaning against each another. *"He caressed my cheek and arm, a bit clumsily, and played with my hair. Most of the time our heads were touching. How I suddenly made the right move-ment, I don't know, but before we went downstairs,*

he gave me a kiss, through my hair, half on my left cheek and half on my ear. I tore downstairs without looking back, and I long so much for today." (April 16, 1944)

3 Anne wonders if her parents approve of her kissing a boy. He is seventeen-and-a-half, she's almost fifteen. She actually thinks they don't, but she decides to do exactly as she pleases. *"It's so peaceful and safe, lying in his arms and dreaming, it's so thrilling to feel his cheek against mine, it's so wonderful to know there's someone waiting for me. But, and there is a but, will Peter want to leave it at this?"* (April 17, 1944)

"Saturday night I asked Peter whether he thinks I shoul tell Father about us. After we'd discussed it, he said he thought I should. As soon as I came downstairs I went with Father to get some water. While we were on the

2

1

3

airs, I said: 'Father, I'm sure you've gathered that
hen Peter and I are together, we don't exactly sit at
opposite ends of the room. Do you think that's wrong?'
ather paused before answering: 'No, I don't think it's
rong. But Anne, when you're living so close together,
s we do, you have to be careful.' We talked some
ore and agreed that Father would speak to him too."
May 2, 1944)

nne's father talks to Peter. Peter tells Anne that Otto
afraid that they will end up falling in love with each
her, but Peter says that he reassured Otto that they
ould keep it under control. *"Father wants me to stop
oing upstairs so often, but I don't want to. Not just
ecause I like being with Peter, but because I've said
rust him. I do trust him, and I want to prove it to him,
ut I'll never be able to if I stay downstairs out of
strust. No, I'm going!"* (May 2, 1944)

As time goes by Anne begins to distance herself from Peter. She sees that Peter is more in need of tenderness than she is. *"He still blushes every evening when he gets his goodnight kiss, and then begs for another one. Am I merely a better substitute for Krauty? I don't mind. He's so happy, just knowing somebody loves him. After my laborious conquest, I've distanced myself a little from the situation, but you mustn't think my love has cooled. Peter's a sweetheart, but I've tightly closed the door to my inner self."* (May 19, 1944)

"Sometimes I think my terrible longing for him was overexaggerated. But that's not true, because if I'm unable to go to his room for a day or two, I long for him as desperately as I ever did. Peter is kind and good, and yet I can't deny that he's disappointed me in many ways. I especially don't care for his dislike of religion,

his table conversations and various things of that nature." (June 13, 1944)

Anne is quite aware of the fact that she has "conquered" Peter instead of the opposite. Due to a need for simple contact intimacies occurred, which on second thought she finds inappropriate. *"We talked about the most private things, but we haven't yet touched upon the things closest to my heart. Now he's holding on for dear life. I honestly don't see any effective way of shaking him off and getting him back on his own two feet."* (July 15, 1944)

After the infatuation has cooled down a bit, Anne once again returns to writing about herself. Certainly in those last weeks, when she is still in a position to note things in her diary, her thoughts grow even deeper.

"I have one outstanding character trait that must be obvious to anyone who's known me for any length of time: I have a great deal of self-knowledge. In everything I do, I can watch myself as if I were a stranger. Without being biased or making excuses, I can stand across from the everyday Anne and watch what she's doing, both the good and the bad. I condemn myself in so many ways that I'm beginning to realize the truth of Father's adage: 'Every child has to raise itself'." (July 15, 1944)

"So if you're wondering whether it's harder for the adults here than for the children, the answer is: no, it's certainly not. Older people have an opinion about everything and are sure of themselves and their actions. It's twice as hard for us young people to hold onto our opinions at a time when ideals are being shattered and destroyed, when the worst side of huma

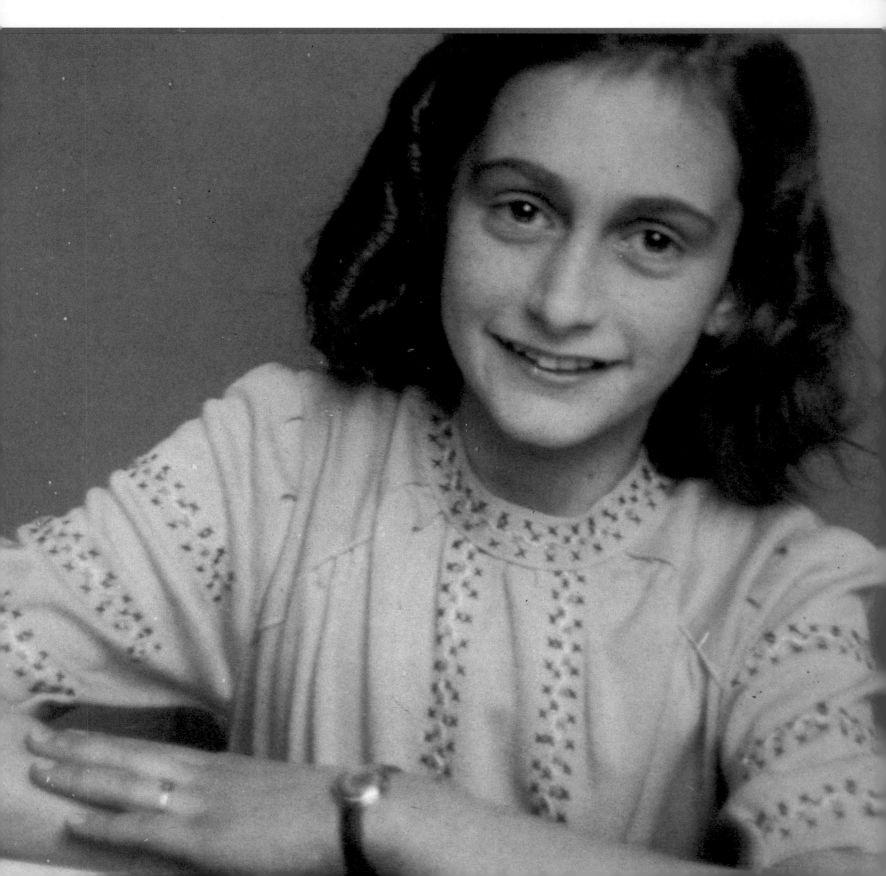

...ature predominates, when everyone has come to
...oubt truth, justice and God." (July 15, 1944)

..." see the world gradually being turned into a waste-
...nd, I hear the ever approaching thunder, which will
...estroy us too, I feel the suffering of millions of people
...nd yet, if I look up into the heavens, I somehow
...el that all this will come right again, that also this
...avagery will stop, that there will be peace and
...anquility in the world once again. Until that time,
...must hold onto my ideals. Perhaps the day will come
...hen I'll still be able to realize them!" (July 15, 1944)

...vo weeks later, on Tuesday August 1, 1944, Anne writes
... her diary for the last time.

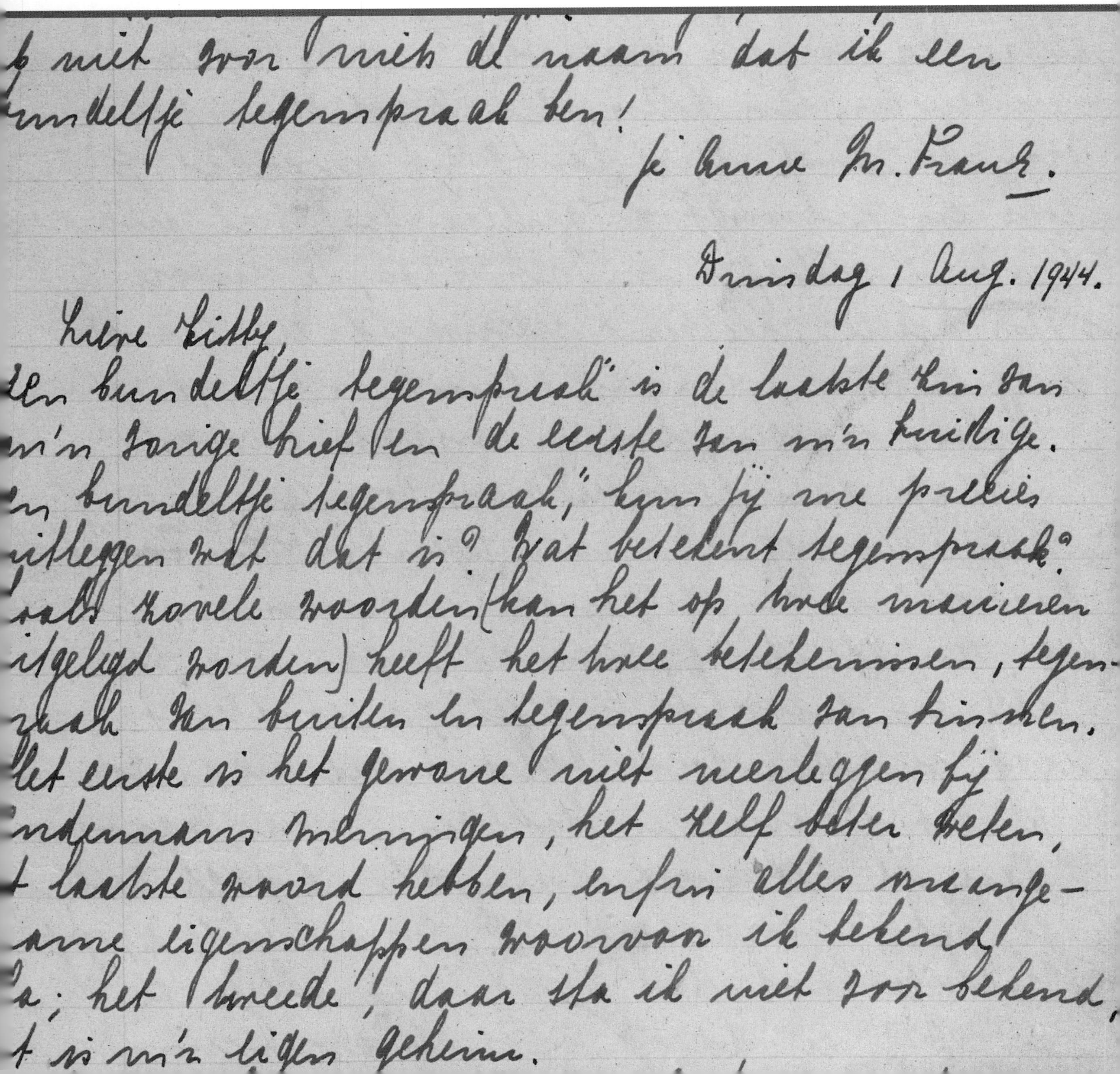

[handwritten diary page, in Dutch]

...p niet voor niets de naam dat ik een
...ndeltje tegenspraak ben!

je Anne M. Frank.

Dinsdag 1 Aug. 1944.

Liefste Kitty,

"Een bundeltje tegenspraak" is de laatste zin van
m'n vorige brief en de eerste van m'n huidige.
"Een bundeltje tegenspraak," kun jij me precies
uitleggen wat dat is? Wat betekent tegenspraak?
Zoals zovele woorden (kan het op twee manieren
uitgelegd worden) heeft het twee betekenissen, tegenspraak van buiten en tegenspraak van binnen.
Het eerste is het gewone niet neerleggen bij
andermans meningen, het zelf beter weten,
het laatste woord hebben, enfin alle onaange-
name eigenschappen waarvoor ik bekend
sta; het tweede, daar sta ik niet voor bekend
dat is m'n eigen geheim.

Jo Kleiman: "On August 4, 1944, the *SD* (German Security Service of the SS) accompanied by three detectives and *SS-Oberstabsfeldwebel* Silberbauer conducted a raid. They had apparently been well-informed, forced my colleague with three guns pointed at him to show them the secret quarters where they arrested both families (8 people). Also my colleague and myself were taken away with them."

Otto Frank: "It was around ten-thirty. I was upstairs by the Van Pelses in Peter's room and I was helping him with his schoolwork, I didn't hear anything. And when I did hear something, I didn't pay any attention to it. Peter had just finished an English dictation and I had just said 'But Peter, in English double is spelled with only one b!'"

"I was showing him the mistake in the dictation when suddenly someone came running up the stairs. The stairs were squeaking, I stood up, because it was still early in the morning and everyone was supposed to be quiet – then the door opened and a man was standing right in front of us with a gun in his hand and it was pointed at us. The man was in plain clothes."

"Peter and I put up our hands. The man had us walk in front of him and ordered us to go downstairs, and he walked behind us with the pistol. Downstairs everyone was gathered. My wife, the children, the Van Pelses stood there with their hands n the air. Then Pfeffer came in, and behind him were still more strangers. In the

middle of the room there was someone from the *Grüne Polizei* (Green Police).

He was studying our faces."

"They then asked us where we kept our valuables? I pointed to the closet by the

wall, where I had stored a small wooden chest. The man from the *Grüne Polizei*

took the box, looked all around him and grabbed Anne's briefcase. He turned it

upside down and shook everything inside it out; there were papers lying all over

the wooden floor – notebooks and loose pages. He proceeded to put all the

valuable things in the briefcase and shut it."

"Then he said: 'Get Ready. Everyone must be back here in five minutes.'

The Van Pelses went upstairs to get their knapsacks, Anne and Pfeffer went to

their room, and I took my knapsack which was hanging on the wall. Suddenly the

man from the *Grüne Polizei* was standing fixated by my wife's bed staring at a

locker that was between the bed and the window and he said loudly: 'Where did

you get this?' He was referring to a gray footlocker with metal strips, like all of

us had during World War One, and on the lid was written : Reserve Lieutenant

Otto Frank. I answered: 'It belongs to me' 'What do you mean?' 'I was an officer'

That really confused him. He stared at me and asked: 'Why didn't you come

forward?' I bit my lip. 'They certainly would have taken that into consideration,

man. You would have been sent you to Theresienstadt.' I was silent. I just looked

at him. Then he said: 'You can take your time...'"

Miep Gies: "It was August 4th. It was quiet in the office. We were working and I happened to look up. The door opened and a small man entered. He pointed the revolver in his hand at me and said: 'Stay seated! Don't move!' Of course, I was frozen with fear. He closed the door and left again. I couldn't see or hear what happened after that because I was ordered to stay at my desk. Later I heard everyone coming downstairs, very slowly. They had been able to pack in the meantime. I wasn't allowed to go to the window, I had to stay in my seat. And I did that. Afterwards Bep and I went upstairs to the bedroom of the Franks. And there we saw Anne's diary lying on the ground. 'Let's pick it up,' I said. Because Bep stood there looking around in a daze. I said: 'Pick it up, pick it up, let's get out of here,' because we were so frightened! We went downstairs and there we were, Bep and I. 'Now what Bep?' Then she said: 'You're the oldest. You should keep it.' That seemed okay."

Victor Kugler: "I heard a commotion and opened the door to my office to see what was going on. I saw four police officers, one was wearing a Gestapo uniform 'Who's in charge here,' he snapped at me? I answered that I was. 'Let me see the rest of the building!' I showed him all the spaces. Then we went upstairs and were standing on the landing by the bookcase. My heart was beating very fast. The three Dutch policemen were already busy trying to open the bookcase. The moment that I had feared for years had arrived. One of the police officers pointed his gun at me and ordered me go first. The others followed behind also with their pistols drawn. The first person I saw was Mrs. Frank. I whispered 'Gestapo,' to her. She sat completely still and seemed to be in shock. The others were coming downstairs from the other floors. Margot was very upset, she was crying softly."

Karl Joseph Silberbauer

In 1948, the police conduct an initial investigation into the betrayal and arrest of those in hiding. Jo Kleiman, Miep Gies, and Victor Kugler identify the Dutch *SD*-detectives as Gezinus Gringhuis and Willem Grootendorst. They are sentenced to life imprisonment. The two men say they can't remember anything about the arrest, but they do mention the name of the Austrian Karl Joseph Silberbauer, who led the action. He, himself, is interrogated during a later investigation in 1964. He declares: "I received a telephone call from my superior, with the message that someone had provided a tip about people in hiding on the Prinsengracht. I went along with a few men. There was a man working in the warehouse who responded to the question of where the Jews were hidden by pointing upstairs with his finger. We went to the second floor, where one of the supervisors of the business was working. He was immediately interrogated by one of the Dutch detectives. When he could no longer deny it, he finally pointed out the hiding place of the Jews. I admit that I entered that Annex with my pistol drawn." Silberbauer still remembers the conversation he had with Otto Frank, who had been an officer during the World War One: "He also told me," so I recall, "that he and his family, which included his daughter Anne, had spent two years in the hiding place. Because I found that hard to believe, he pointed to the pencil marks, the ones that were made by the doorpost to keep track of how much Anne had grown during the time they were in hiding."

Around one o'clock in the afternoon, an enclosed truck drives up in front of the building. The eight people in hiding, Victor Kugler, and Jo Kleiman are loaded into the truck. They are brought to the *SD*-prison on Euterpestraat. Miep Gies and Bep Voskuijl are left behind on the Prinsengracht.

After the Arrest

"The English radio says they're being gassed. I feel terribly upset."

October 9, 1942

The Shoah

On August 4, 1944, a vehicle carrying ten prisoners (the eight people in hiding and two male helpers) rides to the *Sicherheitsdienst* (SD or Bureau of the German Security Service of the SS) on Euterpestraat in Amsterdam. After a short interrogation, Jo Kleiman and Victor Kugler – the two helpers – are brought to the prison on Amstelveenseweg by the Germans. They are held there until September 7, 1944. There is no hearing. After four days in yet another Amsterdam prison, they are relocated to the Amersfoort transit camp. Kleiman's stomach ulcers begin hemorrhaging in the camp and this leads to his release on September 18th. At the end of September, Kugler is sent to do heavy labor with other prisoners in Zwolle and later in Wageningen. He escapes at the beginning of April 1945. Heavy penalties are attached to aiding and abetting Jews. Still, in everyday practice the enforcement of this is quite arbitrary. Miep Gies and Bep Voskuijl are not arrested. Apparently, the male arresting officers cannot imagine that these women were actually involved. They keep the business running.

The Helpers

1 The headquarters of the *Sicherheitsdienst* (German Security Service and Security Police) on Euterpestraa This building also houses the Security Service jail. Miep Gies visits the prison a few days after the arrest to see if she can do anything for the imprisoned inhabitants of the Secret Annex and the helpers. Unfortunately, she is unsuccessful.

2 Jo Kleiman's Red Cross form, filled in on October 14, 1945. Kleiman says that he was arrested "due to hiding and caring for eight Jewish people". The only person from the arresting team explicitly named in his statement is *Oberscharführer* Karl Joseph Silberbauer, the head of the Security Office. The three plainclothe Dutch Nazis worked for the *Sicherheitsdienst* and the Central Office for Jewish Emigration. Silberbauer, a member of the SS since 1939, begins working in the Netherlands in November 1943.

1

3

4

e prison on Amstelveenseweg. After the war, Victor
ugler points out the cell where he was held: B3-11.
Kleiman occupies the next cell. Six people on average
habit a cell meant for one person. Victor Kugler and
Kleiman are imprisoned here for about five weeks.
ey stay in contact by ticking signals on the heating
bes and exchanging notes during fresh air breaks.

n September 11, 1944, Kleiman and Kugler arrive
the *Polizeiliches Durchgangslager Amersfoort*
mersfoort Police Transit Camp). They are considered
tisocial prisoners and as an indication of this receive
ed circle on the back of their coats. The conditions
the camp are very severe. The Jewish prisoners are
eated the worst. Thirty-five thousand people in total
e imprisoned in this camp during the war.

ctor Kugler's detailed registration in Camp

Amersfoort. The stamp shows that on September 26,
1944, he is assigned to the *Arbeitseinsatz* (forced labor
in Nazi-Germany). The stated reason for his arrest
is *Judenbegünstigung* or 'helping Jews'.

6 Victor Kugler's forged identity card, which he has
made after his escape.

*"I was imprisoned in jails, concentration camps and
work camps for eight months, and I've been in many
dangerous situations, such as a grenade attack by the
British near Wageningen. Finally I was 'selected' to go
to Germany. I knew exactly what this meant. When our
group of about six hundred people was attacked by
a British Spitfire near the German border, I managed
to escape. A German farmer gave me shelter for a few
days, afterwards I went home by bike."* (Victor Kugler,
around 1970)

7 Registration card of Jo Kleiman in Camp Amersfoort.
The card, which is damaged immediately after
the Liberation, states: "Arrival: September 11, 1944.
Departure: September 18, 1944 to *Heimatort* (released
to home address)." When Kleiman is released after
six weeks of imprisonment, the people in hiding are
already in Auschwitz. After his return, Kleiman resumes
his work on the Prinsengracht. Miep Gies and Bep
Voskuijl show him the diary papers of Anne Frank.

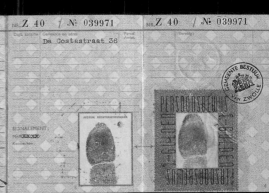

6

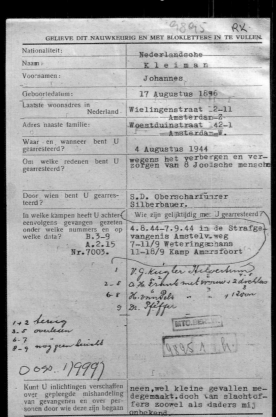

5

2

The people in hiding are kept in the House of Detention on Weteringschans in Amsterdam from August 5-8, 1944. Early in the morning on August 8, 1944 they are taken out of their cell and brought to the central train station. Another group joins them, also Jews arrested because of their Resistance activities or caught while in hiding. The prisoners travel by passenger train, but as "penalty cases", to Westerbork. During this trip, for the first time in a long time, they see the summery landscape. After a few hours of traveling they arrive in Westerbork, located on the heathland in Drenthe, a province of the Netherlands close to the German border. In this transit camp, the stress of impending deportation continually hangs in the air.

1 In the late 1930's, the Dutch government has the camp in Westerbork built in order to house Jewish refugees fleeing Nazi Germany. On July 1, 1942, the Nazi occupying force turns it into a *Polizeiliches Durch-gangslager*, a police transit camp enroute to the camp in Germany and Poland. In 1942 and 1943, most of the Jews living in the Netherlands are deported via this camp "to the East". Exactly what this destination enta is not known to them. By 1944, the camp primarily houses people who have been spared deportation or those who have been arrested while in hiding, like Ann and the others.

2 The S-Barrack # 67 at Westerbork houses the "penalt cases", who wear a red piece of fabric on their camp clothing. In retrospect, the situation of the former inhabitants of the Secret Annex does not differ much from others in the camp. The De Winter family, the

The People in Hiding

1

2

3

...ouple Deliema, and Frieda Menco are all arrested ...the beginning of August just like the Frank family. ...hey all live in the same barrack. Later on they talk ...bout their encounter. *"On August 5, 1944, the ...ermans were informed about our hiding place. ...hey arrested us, put us in jail, and then transported ...s to Westerbork. We had to sort batteries in the ...enalty barracks. There we met the Frank family, the ...ther couple, their son Peter and the other gentleman, ...ho had all been together in one house in Amsterdam. ...e talked a lot about our experiences. They had been ...rrested one day earlier. We tried to help each other, ...o keep our spirits up."* (Rose Deliema)

...or the inhabitants of the Secret Annex, internment ...the camp on the heathland of Drenthe means that for ...e first time in two years they once again have contact ...ith other people and with the open air. Frieda Menco

can also remember the relief at being able to go out-side again at Westerbork, after a lengthy and oppres-sive period of hiding marked by starvation. *"Westerbork was the best time of the war for me. I had been so hungry during the hiding period. At Westerbork, I had more space to walk than in the previous two years. That must also have been the case for the Frank family. We worked during the day and were fed. After two months, we almost began to believe that we wouldn't be transported."* (Frieda Menco)

4   The prisoners from the penalty barrack carry out work for the German weapons industry. It is grimy, unhealthy work because of the exposure to chemicals. *"I ended up working with the batteries,"* tells Bloeme Evers-Emden, who met the Frank Family in Westerbork. She knew Margot quite well from school. *"It was such dirty work. You had to crack open old batteries and

inside them there was a type of metal that you had to remove. I don't know what they did with it. You were black from top to toe when you came out of there. You could go and shower but you couldn't get clean."*

5   The registration cards of the Frank family and the Van Pels family from the official Registry of the Municipality of Westerbork. The handwritten notations on the cards were made by Red Cross workers who after the war collected and distributed information about deportees. The typed and stamped information dates from 1944. Fritz Pfeffer's registration card is lost. On these preprinted cards, a Westerbork town official typed and stamped information about the new camp arrivals, complete with date of birth and last official address. The transport date out of Westerbork is stamped all the way at the bottom: September 3, 1944. To "Abroad" cloaks the real destination.

4

5

Life in Westerbork transit camp revolves around the deportation train. From the summer of 1942 until the spring of 1943, a train departs "to the East" almost every Tuesday, each time crammed with hundreds, even thousands of people. At a later date, the transports decrease in both frequency and size. Experiencing unbearable tension, everyone in the camps awaits the reading of the new list of deportees. In total, 100,000 Jews are deported from Westerbork. About 245 Roma and Sinti (Gypsies) are also deported from Westerbork. Initially, the precise destinations are not known. Most of the trains go to the extermination camps Sobibor and Auschwitz. Bergen-Belsen and Theresienstadt are other destinations.

Westerbork Transit Camp

1 Part of the list of the 83rd *Judentransport* (transport of Jews) from Westerbork to "the East", on September 3, 1944. This transport, which included the inhabitants of the Secret Annex, was the last transport from Westerbork to Auschwitz. There are 1019 people on this train; 498 men, 442 women and 79 children, all Jewish according to Nazi criteria. Frieda Brommet; Rachel van Amerongen; Rozette (Ronnie) van Cleef; Bloeme Emden; Judik, Manus and Rosa de Winter; and Sally and Rose Deliema are also on the list. These women are some of the few survivors and later they describe the life of Anne, Margot, Edith and Otto in the camps.

2 People who are being deported desperately try to send last messages to their families. This letter is written by Judik de Winter, also on behalf of her mother Rosa and her father Manus, one day before their departure.

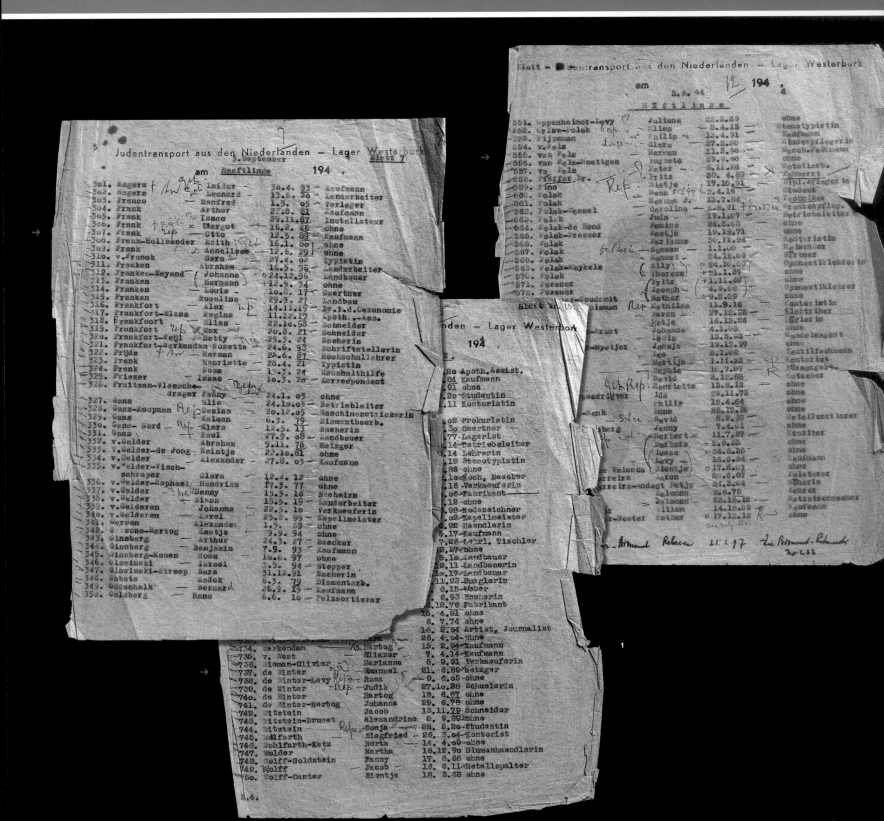

"Dear folks, Tomorrow, September 3rd, we're going to be transported; to where we don't know, to the East for sure. We are in good spirits and still fit and will do our best to come through this. The situation here is dreadful." Judik, Manus and Rosa de Winter send this letter to Judik's aunt. They have no idea what will happen to them "in the East". Later, in Auschwitz, Rosa de Winter comes in contact with Edith Frank.

transport departing from Westerbork. A few people are successful in escaping from the train that leaves on September 3rd. Using a saw, they make a hole in the wooden floor of the train boxcar shortly after departing. Five people lower themselves through the opening. Although they are injured, all five survive. When the guards on the train realize what has happened, they move the remaining prisoners from this boxcar to other freight cars.

4 The train departing Westerbork. The girl wearing the kerchief is Settela Steinbach. She is a Gypsy of Sinti descent and for this reason is deported to Auschwitz, where she is murdered.

5 This signboard was on the side of the train going from Westerbork to Auschwitz. The train journey takes a few days. In closed boxcars without windows, with far too many people in a much too small space, with hardly any water and food, without fresh air and without toilets. *"I think of darkness when I think of that train trip. Too many people. Not enough space. Luggage. No space to lie down. Three days of sitting. Every now and again standing. We had no idea where we were going, where we would stop and how long it would take."* (Frieda Menco)

"Mrs. Frank had smuggled a blue overall on board and by the light of a flashlight was unstitching the red piece of fabric. Many people, also the Frank girls, slept against their mother or father, everyone was dead tired." (Lenie de Jong-van Naarden)

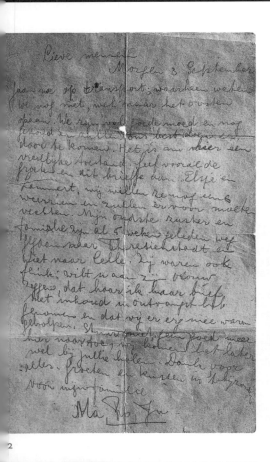

3

5

"I can no longer talk about how I felt when my family arrived on the train platform in Auschwitz and we were forcibly separated from each other."

Otto Frank, 1979

Auschwitz-Birkenau

Arrival and "selection" of Hungarian Jews
in Auschwitz-Birkenau, May 1944.

Of the eight people in hiding, Hermann van Pels is the first to die. He arrives with the others in Auschwitz on the night of September 5, 1944. A "selection" takes place immediately. The men are separated from the women. Children younger than fifteen, the elderly, people who are weak and sick are immediately gassed. The others, including for the time being all the inhabitants of the Secret Annex, are transferred to work camps. Here they come in contact with a system aimed at dehumanizing people: their heads are shaven bald, they receive camp clothes, and a number is tattooed on their arm. The male Secret Annex inhabitants receive a number between B-9108 and B-9365. A prisoner is referred to by his or her number. Hermann van Pels is assigned to a commando unit (forced-labor group) that works outdoors. A few weeks later he is gassed. At that time, he is 54 years old. The precise date of his death is unknown.

Hermann van Pels

1 Registration card of Hermann van Pels, from the administration of the Jewish Council in Westerbork. After the Liberation, the Dutch Red Cross confiscated the registration-card file boxes from Westerbork to be able to provide information about deportees. Written on this card in red pencil is the date S 3-9-44, on which Herman van Pels was transported from Westerbork to Auschwitz.

"I will never forget that moment when the 17-year-old Peter van Pels and I saw a group of selected men. Peter's father was among the group. They were marched away. Two hours later a cart with their clothes on it went by." (Otto Frank)

2 The entry gate to Auschwitz. The inscription *"Arbeit Macht Frei"* ('Work Sets Us Free') fits in with the Nazi strategy of depicting all the camps as work camps.

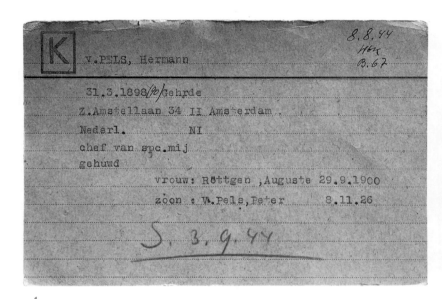

1

3

ermann and Peter van Pels, Otto Frank and Fritz
effer end-up in Blocks 1 or 2 of this camp. Immedi-
ely upon the arrival of a train, the SS selects all those
ople who are judged fit enough to work. They have
perform heavy labor, each and every day from six in
e morning until five-thirty in the evening.

klon B Gas canisters. Auschwitz-Birkenau is an exter-
ination camp. The mass murder here is organized
the Nazis in an industrialized fashion. In September
41, the Nazis begin using gas chambers. The Shoah
the genocide of the Jews, the murder of a people on
unprecedented scale. In Auschwitz-Birkenau alone,
e Nazis killed more than one million Jews. Exact
ures are not known because the people who were
ssed immediately upon their arrival were never regis-
red. After the war, the camp commander, Rudolf
öss, states both a figure of 1.3 million and 2.5 million

victims of Auschwitz. The last gassing in Auschwitz-
Birkenau occurs in the beginning of November 1944.
Three weeks earlier on October 7, 1944, one of the gas
chambers is partially desstroyed during a prison revolt.
With the approach of the Soviet Army in November
1944, the gas chambers and crematoria are torn down
to wipe out any evidence of mass murder.

"Mr. van Pels ended up with his son Peter, Otto, and
Fritz Pfeffer together in the same barrack. Every day he
went to do the work he was assigned. After a few weeks,
in October or November, he severely injured his
thumbs and he asked to be excused from work the next
day. He was then attached to group working in-and-
around the barracks. On that very same day men were
selected from the barracks to be gassed. Mr. van Pels
was among them. He was never seen again." (Fritzi
Frank from a story told to her by Otto Frank, 1990)

4 Auschwitz-Birkenau, May 1944. All the baggage
and clothing belonging to those who are murdered in
the gas chambers is sorted by the other prisoners.
It is a much desired job assignment. Often something
edible or something that can be bartered is found
among all the belongings. Yet it remains risky to take
something for yourself. If a guard catches a prisoner,
brutal mishandling or another severe punishment
follows. Prisoners are also set to work emptying the gas
chambers and burning the bodies in the crematoria.

Fritz Pfeffer is just one of the prisoners transferred from Auschwitz to another camp. Prisoners continue to hope that life will be better somewhere else. Fritz Pfeffer also harbors these same hopes. In October 1944, he signs up for a doctor's transport leaving Auschwitz. He ends up in Neuengamme, a concentration camp near Hamburg. This camp has more than eighty outdoor commando units operating; sixty for male prisoners and twenty for female prisoners. All are engaged in doing heavy forced labor. The abominable working conditions, the poor clothing, the inadequate nutrition, the lack of health care and hygiene, and abuse by the SS and camp guards result in the death of many prisoners. These deaths are part and parcel of the deliberate policy of the Nazis to kill people through the use of forced labor. Fritz Pfeffer dies in Neuengamme's sick-bay barrack on December 20, 1944 at the age of fifty-five.

Fritz Pfeffer

1   Fritz Pfeffer's card from the records of the Jewish Council in Westerbork.

2   In the prisoner's Death Registry of Neuengamme, Fritz Pfeffer's death is noted: "Jew 64971-German Nationality; Pfeffer, Fritz; Born April 30, 1889; Died: December 20, 1944; Time: 9 o'clock; Cause of death: enterocolitis." Enteritis and colitis are intestinal diseases. These sicknesses can normally be cured quite easily but in the concentration camps they are a major cause of death. The Death Registry is kept up to date by the prisoners who work in the sick-bay barrack. Practically the entire archive of Neuengamme, including all evidence of the massive amount of deaths, is destroyed by the Nazis. The only remaining evidence is saved by the prisoners themselves.

1

6

rced laborers working on the Dove-Elbe canal. e heavy digging work on this canal is done by isoners from Neuengamme. They are systematically miliated and violently mishandled during this work. e economic value of the work is only of secondary portance to the Nazis. The killing off of certain popu- ion groups is the primary objective. The prisoners m various camps mostly do work for the weapons dustry. Management of the camps is in the hands the *SS*.

euengamme, around 1941.

nnihilation by Labor" is a key part of the concen- tion camp system of the Nazis from 1938-1945. cording to the them, only people belonging to the -called Aryan race are allowed to live in Germany. nly then will there be a "healthy German people".

Those who don't belong to this group or who resist these ideas are expelled, persecuted and murdered. This includes Jews, Roma and Sinti (Gypsies) the disabled, political opponents, homosexuals, Jehovah's Witnesses and others.

5   The sick-bay barrack in the *Stammlager* (main camp) of Neuengamme concentration camp, the place where Fritz Pfeffer dies. In these barracks, exhausted and starved prisoners all with different illnesses lie crammed together on wooden plank beds. There is no medical care. The medics can only take in the sick and have the dead taken away.

6   Charlotte Kaletta, as Fritz Pfeffer's "fiancée", fills in this card in an attempt to get more information about him from the Red Cross. She wants to know what has happened to her partner. The last news she has about

him dates from October 1, 1944. She has probably heard from Otto Frank that on that date Fritz suppo- sedly traveled on a "special doctor's transport with 60 doctors from Auschwitz to Gdańsk," as she writes on the card. By the end of 1945, she knows that her fiancé has died. Charlotte marries Fritz Pfeffer posthumously on April 5, 1953.

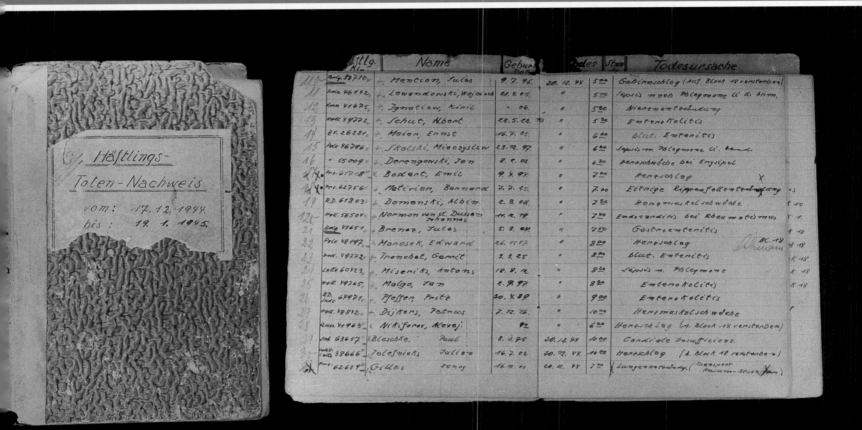

Edith Frank, her daughters, and the other new female arrivals spend their first few days in Auschwitz "in quarantine". The arms of the 212 Dutch women from the September 3, 1944 transport are tattooed with numbers ranging from A-25060 to A-25271. After the quarantine, most of the women – so probably including Edith, Margot and Anne – are assigned to commando units (forced-labor groups). The Frank women end up in a barrack with many other Dutch women. Survivors later relate that there is a very strong bond between the mother and her daughters. Apparently, the bickering between Anne and Edith has been relegated to the past. At the end of October, when a large number of Dutch women are transferred to a labor camp in Liebau (Upper Silesia) Edith remains behind with her sick daughters. A few days later a new selection takes place. Margot and Anne are put on a transport to Bergen-Belsen concentration camp and Edith must say goodbye to her daughters. At the end of November, Edith ends up in the sick-bay barrack. She dies there on January 6, 1945 at the age of forty-four.

Edith Frank-Holländer

1 Edith Frank's card from the records of the Jewish Council in Westerbork.

"I spoke to Mrs. Frank who was with Margot; Anne was somewhere else, she had Krätze (scabies) and had to be in isolation. Therefore Anne couldn't come with our group and Mrs. Frank said: 'So of course, we are going to go with her.' Margot repeated these same words once again." (Bloeme Evers-Emden)

"I was in the Krätzeblock (one of the scabies barracks) with Anne and Margot. Our mothers had pinched food wherever they could, in order to feed us. They had dug a hole under the barrack. So they called to us. And then I went and got the food, a piece of bread or some meat or sausage, and then we shared that with each other." (Ronnie Goldstein-van Cleef)

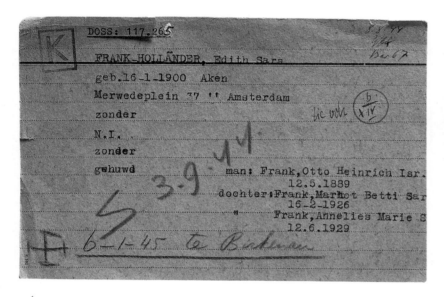

1

3

Appell (roll-call) of Hungarian Jews, May 1944.
the prisoners have to get up every morning at 3:30
M. and stand outside on the central courtyard in rows
five in order to be to be counted. This usually takes
urs, and afterwards many of them have to go to work.
October 2, 1944, a total of 11,506 of the 26,230
soners in the women's camp are working as forced
borers. The rest is either in quarantine, sick, or
aiting transport to another camp.

*Constant selections... Edith, a good acquaintance
mine, is also with me, she had to give up her two
ughters, 15 and 18 years old. We comfort each other
d become friends, we are preparing ourselves for
e worst."* (Rosa de Winter, 1945)

schwitz-Birkenau shortly after the Liberation, early
45. A photo taken by the Russian army.

4 *Escape from the Gas Chamber* is the title of the book
that Rosa de Winter writes at the end of 1945 about her
experiences in Auschwitz. Rosa de Winter and Edith
Frank become friends at Auschwitz-Birkenau in Camp
B-II-B block 29. They are transferred to Camp A, block
4a at the beginning of November 1944, where for the
time being, they do not have to work.

5 Auschwitz-Birkenau 1945.

A few weeks later Edith Frank and Rosa de Winter are
transferred again. *"Edith and I are still with each other...
Edith has taken ill, has a high fever. I want her to go to
the Ambulance (hospital). Though there is great fear
of being gassed because every week Dr. Mengele goes
to the sick-bay barracks to pick out those women whom
in his opinion are too thin to be left alive. Despite everything, I bring Edith there. She has a fever of 105°F (41°C)*

*and is immediately admitted to the Revier (sick-bay
barracks)."* This is at the end of November. Shortly
thereafter, Rosa also becomes so ill that she ends up
in another barrack for sick prisoners. At the beginning
of January 1945, the temparature drops to minus
70°F (-40°C). On January 6, 1945, in the freezing cold,
Edith succumbs to her illness. Rosa manages to survive
in the sick-bay barrack where she is liberated by the
Russians on January 27, 1945. During her return trip to
the Netherlands, she meets Otto Frank and tells him
that his wife has died.

*"One morning new patients arrive. Suddenly,
I recognize Edith, she has come from a another ward
of sick-bay barracks. She is but a mere shadow of
herself. A few days later she dies, totally worn out."*
(Rosa de Winter)

At first, Margot Frank is together with her sister and mother in Auschwitz. At the end of October 1944, the Soviet forces advance on Poland, where the camp is located. The Nazis bring as many prisoners as possible back to Germany, especially those prisoners who are still able to work. Margot and Anne Frank are selected for transport to Bergen-Belsen. They supposedly leave Auschwitz by train on October 28, 1944, in boxcars squeezed full with 1,306 other women, enroute to Bergen-Belsen. This could have also occurred on November 1, 1944, in an evacuation transport with 634 other women. A train journey of four days; once again in freight cars crammed full of people, with little food or water. From the train station in Celle, the prisoners have to walk many miles to the Bergen-Belsen camp. When the prisoners from Auschwitz arrive, Bergen-Belsen is already more than full. The conditions there are awful, there is a shortage of everything, and contagious diseases are running rampant. A few months later, in March 1945, Margot Frank dies of typhus and deprivation in Bergen-Belsen. She has just turned nineteen years old. The exact date of her death is unknown.

Margot Frank

1 Margot Frank's card from the records of the Jewish Council in Westerbork.

2 The first few days at Bergen-Belsen, Margot and Anne are housed in tents. By August 1944, the Bergen-Belsen camp was already so overcrowded that a separate encampment was set up to accommodate prisoners evacuated from other camps. All of the tents on the *Lüneburgerheide* (on the heathlands between Celle and Lüneburg) collapse during a severe storm in November 1944. Anne and Margot are transferred along with the other women to another part of the camp. This photograph is made by the British army, shortly after the liberation of the camp on April 15, 1945.

"The two Frank girls were inseparable, just like my sister and I. We met up with them again in Bergen-Belsen. At first they didn't want to sleep in the tents.

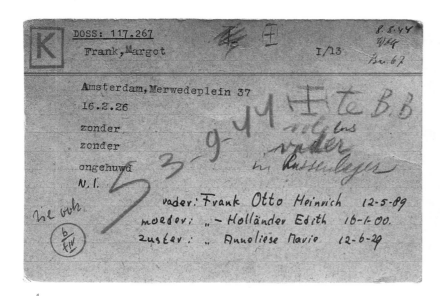

1

3

2

…was dirty inside the tents and it smelled awful."
…entje Brilleslijper, who was also evacuated from
…uschwitz to Bergen-Belsen.)

…o patients suffering from typhus in the hospital at
…rgen-Belsen, April 20, 1945. Even after the liberation
…the camp, many people still die.

…omen's barrack in Bergen-Belsen shortly after the
…eration of the camp. About 8,000 women from
…schwitz-Birkenau arrive in Bergen-Belsen during
…ctober and November 1944. At the time of its liber-
…on, the camp still houses about 56,000 people who
…e starving and ill. Ten-thousand bodies have not yet
…en buried. A total of 80,000 people die in this camp.

…met Anne and her sister, Margot, again in the
…rracks. I almost didn't recognize the Frank girls

because their hair was cut so short. And they were
so cold just like the rest of us. It was winter and you
didn't have proper clothing. They had the worst spot in
the barracks, down below next to the door which was
constantly opened and closed. You heard them continually screaming: 'Close the door, close the door!'
and that yelling grew weaker with each and every
day. You could literally see them dying."
(Rachel van Amerongen-Frankfoorder)

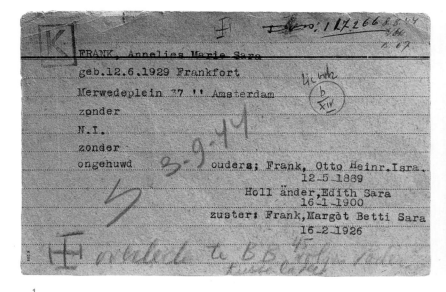

During the selection on the train platform in Auschwitz, Anne Frank escapes the gas chambers. Along with Margot, Edith and other new arrivals she is first placed "in quarantine". Following this, the prisoners are usually appointed to a commando unit. An opportunity to rest after working does not really exist. The barracks are filled with wooden plank beds crammed full with people. The endless roll-calls are deathly tiring. After a few weeks Anne falls ill. Together with Margot, they are admitted to a separate barrack housing sick prisoners. Here the risk of being selected for the gas chambers is very high. At the end of October or beginning of November 1944, the Frank sisters are evacuated to the German concentration camp Bergen-Belsen. Their mother, Edith, remains behind. From the well-organized death factory of Auschwitz they arrive at a huge, poorly organized, chaotic camp. Thirst and hunger are pervasive in Bergen-Belsen. There is no adequate sanitation. Epidemics claim thousands of victims. Anne survives for a little over four months in Bergen-Belsen, finally succumbing to typhus and deprivation. She dies in March 1945 at the age of fifteen, just a few weeks before the liberation of the camp and a few days after Margot dies. The exact date of Anne's death is not known.

Anne Frank

1 Anne Frank's card from the records of the Jewish Council in Westerbork.

"Perhap Auschwitz was worse with regard to the number of dead, but you saw it less there. Here in Belsen, you felt the dead. It was also closer to home, near Holland. I saw Anne Frank here, sick and with typhus. You could tell from her appearance, her eyes. (Rachel van Amerongen-Frankfoorder)

2 Bergen-Belsen, 1945. After the liberation, 600-1000 people are counted by the British in some barracks meant for 100 prisoners. The Bergen-Belsen camp is originally a German army camp and beginning in 194 it is used to house French, Belgian, and later on, also Russian prisoners of war. Thirty-thousand Russian prisoners die in the camp. Beginning in April 1943, so-called tradeable Jews are also interned here: prisoner

1

3

4

2

2

at the Nazis can swap in exchange for Germans. ey are housed in the so-called *Sternlager* ('Star camp', e of the sections of Bergen-Belsen). When the tent campment collapses in November 1944 (because the bad weather) the prisoners in the *Sternlager* e crowded even closer together. An area, fenced off h barbed wire and walled-off with straw, is laid out the middle of the camp to keep the different groups prisoners from communicating with each other. The men from the tent encampment, including Anne d Margot Frank, are housed in four empty barracks the other side of the barbed wire.

annah Goslar, a friend of Anne's from the years fore going into hiding, in a photograph taken at rgen-Belsen in 1996. Beginning in February 1944, nnah is placed in the *Sternlager* and that is where e hears, at a certain moment, that Anne Frank is

with the women in the tent camp. *"So I went to the barbed wire, but that was forbidden and the Germans kept watch from the tower. I waited until it got dark and went there and started to call out. I received an answer from Mrs. van Pels. She said immediately to me: 'You want Anne.' She went to get Anne; Margot was already very sick."* This occurs prior to February 25, 1945, the day Hannah's father dies in the camp. Shortly before her meeting with Anne, Hannah receives a package from the Red Cross. From that package she makes a small packet for Anne.

"All of my friends also contributed something, a glove, a bit of bread, and I threw it over the barbed wire. I suddenly heard a scream, and what had happened, a woman next to Anne had caught the package and didn't want to give it back. Then I tried again and the second time she caught the packet

and that was the last time I spoke to her." (Hannah Goslar)

4 Bergen-Belsen shortly after its liberation. Hannah Goslar: *"Anne thought that her parents were dead. I have always thought if Anne had known that her father was still alive, she would have found the strength to go on living."*

On the train platform in Auschwitz, Gusti van Pels is separated from her husband and son. She probably also loses contact with Edith, Anne and Margot rather quickly. The many thousands of prisoners are split-up into different camps all cordoned off by barbed wire. Gusti van Pels' residence barrack and commando unit in Auschwitz are not known. She is transferred on November 26, 1944 to Bergen-Belsen. Here she sees Margot and Anne Frank once again. Gusti is the one who arranges the meeting between Anne and Hannah Goslar. On February 6, 1945, Gusti is transported again, to the *Raguhn* commando, an outdoor commando unit of Buchenwald concentration camp. She probably works there until *Raguhn* is evacuated and the prisoners are taken to Theresienstadt. Auguste van Pels dies in April or May 1945, on her way to or shortly after arriving in Theresienstadt. At the time of her death, she is forty-four years old.

Auguste van Pels

1 Auguste van Pels's card from the records of the Jewish Council in Westerbork.

2 The registration card of Auguste van Pels-Röttgen from the official Registry of the Municipality of Westerbork. Typed on the card is the date she arrives at the transit camp: August 8, 1944. The stamp showing the date of departure: "September 3, 1944, Abroad" is also clearly visible. On the back of the card, a Red Cross worker has made notations about Auguste van Pels' journey to other concentration camps in Poland and Germany.

3 Transport of prisoners to Theresienstadt, 1942. A small group of women, including Rachel van Amerongen, join the outdoor commando unit of *Raguhn* on February 2, 1945. Just like Auguste van Pels they are selected in Bergen-Belsen to work as slave laborers. Raguhn is situated in eastern Germany,

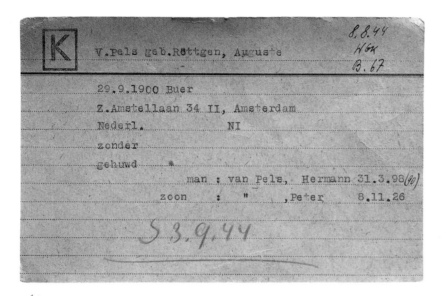

1

3

5

ear Halle, where an airplane factory is located.
achel doesn't remember Auguste van Pels. Rachel
as to work with nine Polish women in a cellar peeling
otatoes. Through that work she is able to regain a bit
 her strength: *"Until that also came to an end and
e were transported again."* (Rachel van Amerongen-
ankfoorder)

*We were about to be liberated and they were trying
 prevent this. Nobody knew where we were being
ken. It was a horrible transport, simply because many
eople didn't have it in them anymore to climb down
ch and every time from the cattle wagon in order
 relieve themselves. Even worse was that there
ere women who didn't have the energy any more to
imb back into the wagons. They stayed behind and
ere never seen again."* (Rachel van Amerongen-
ankfoorder)

4 A barrack in Theresienstadt, not far from Prague.
At first it is considered a "good" camp. German Jews
who fought for their country during World War One
are "favored" and sent to this camp. Also people who
initially have their deportations delayed end up here.
For the eyes of the outside world, the Nazis try to create
the illusion that Theresienstadt is a model camp – an
organized "ghetto" with a school, family life, work and
recreation. By showing the camp to international
observers, the Nazis divert attention away from the
extermination camps in Poland. In 1942, Theresienstadt
becomes a transit camp similar to Westerbork, with
many transports going to Auschwitz.

5 Dachau, May 1945. Just like with so many other people,
the exact date and place of Auguste van Pels' death
is not known. She dies somewhere in Germany or
Czechoslovakia between April 9th and May 8, 1945.

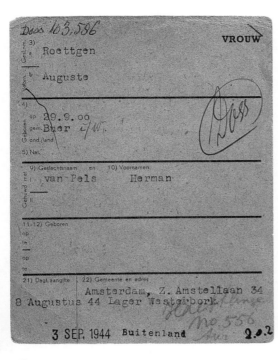

2

2

4

Peter van Pels probably spends a few weeks in Auschwitz together with his father. In October or November 1944 he sees his father being taken off to the gas chamber. Peter works in the postal department, which is less severe than working in one of the outdoor commando units. Because of this job, he sometimes comes across extra food which he shares with Otto Frank and other prisoners. Sometime around January 20, 1945, the advancing Russian army is so close to Auschwitz that the *SS* decides to flee the camp. They have already dismantled the gas chambers in November. They now try to destroy the camp archives and they take prisoners along with them when they leave. During these evacuations, quite often by foot, many prisoners die. The details of Peter van Pels' evacuation journey are not known. He is probably still transported by train or truck, because he arrives in Mauthausen on January 25, 1945. He dies there on May 5, 1945, the day of the Liberation. He is eighteen years old.

Peter van Pels

1 Peter van Pels' card from the records of the Jewish Council in Westerbork.

2 Prisoners from Dachau during a "death march", 1945.

In Auschwitz, Peter van Pels meets Max Stoppelman. Max is the "eldest on the block". Peter knows Stoppelman's mother and tells Max that his mother ha safely gone into hiding in the Netherlands. Max takes Peter under his wing. "He told me that he knew Jan and Miep Gies, and that my mother was still fine. I told him to stick as close to me as possible and that I would try to pull him through. I was going to be transported on January 17, 1945 and I couldn't locate Peter. Perhaps he had already been put on another transport."

3 On January 25, 1945, after a grueling trip, Peter arrives at the infamous Mathausen concentration and exterm

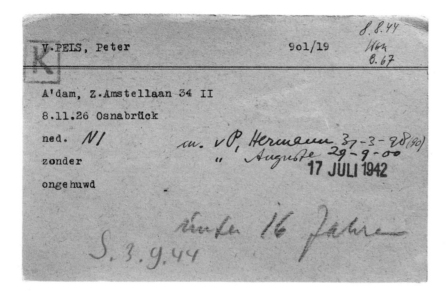

1

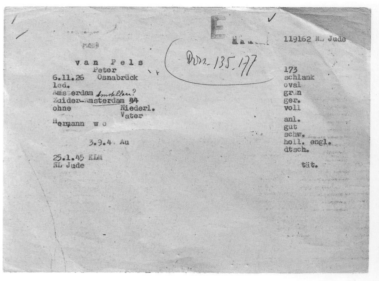

3

5

2

tion camp. A typist places two sheets of paper in
ypewriter used for registering people. The top pre-
inted sheet lists all the needed categories. From this
rm, a supervisor can determine in what capacity
e prisoner can best be used as a (slave) laborer.
he prisoner's number is located in the top right hand
rner: 119162, NL (=Dutch) Jew. Underneath that the
hysical characteristics of Peter are listed: Height: 5'7"
uild: slender. Face: oval. Eyes: green. Nose: straight.
outh: full. Ears: flat against the head. Teeth: good.
air: black. Languages: Dutch, English, German.
pecial characteristics: tattoo (a number tattoo had
ready been assigned to Peter in Auschwitz).

r the carbon copy for Mauthausen's records, the
pist uses an old form dating from 1943. Listed on the
ck of the sheet of paper is Peter's stated profession:
schler (furniture maker). The stamp indicates date of

arrival: January 25, 1945. Peter is placed in quarantine
until January 29, 1945. From January 29th until April 11,
1945, he works for *Quarz*: an outdoor commando unit
from Mauthausen that is also referred to as *Melk*.
The name is indicative of heavy labor in rock quarries,
construction, underground munition works and rocket
factories, and so forth. *Melk* is evacuated in the middle
of April 1945, and the prisoners are returned to the
main camp. Peter then ends up in the sick-bay barrack
in Mauthausen.

5 Prisoners in one of Mauthausen's barracks, May 6,
1945. The Mauthausen camp in Austria is built on the
site of a granite quarry. In 1938 it is already operating.
Also in this camp the Nazis apply the principle of
"Annihilation by Labor." With very heavy labor under
the worst conditions imaginable, in the stone quarries
the Nazis kill – according to estimates – more than

100,000 prisoners. Among them are Poles, Czechs,
Russian prisoners of war, Spanish Republicans, Dutch
Jews, Sinti and Roma (Gypsies), and French, Belgian,
Yugoslavian and Austrian communists. Peter van Pels
is literally worked to death here in the last two months
of his life.

6 On May 5, 1945, the American Army liberates
Mauthausen. These young prisoners are placed in an
Army Field Hospital in order to regain their strength.

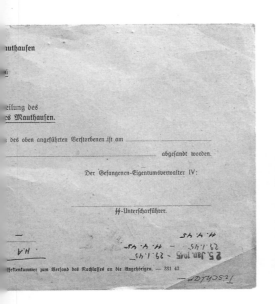

Otto Frank is the only one of the eight people in hiding who survives the camps. Even he cannot explain it. *"I was blessed with luck, and many friends,"* he writes to his mother about this. After enduring several months of heavy labor in one of Auschwitz's outdoor commando units, Otto is finally completely exhausted. Thanks to the intervention of a doctor he ends up in the sick-bay barrack. There certainly isn't any medical care but at least he doesn't have to work anymore. Peter van Pels visits Otto Frank daily and cares for him. He also visits Otto shortly before the evacuation of Auschwitz, sometime around January 20, 1945, and insists that Otto should also come along. But he doesn't have any strength left to make the trip. It is exactly this that leads to his salvation. The Soviet army liberates Auschwitz on January 27, 1945. Otto is one of the 7,560 prisoners that has remained behind. After a journey home lasting several months, he finally arrives back in the Netherlands in June 1945.

Otto Frank

1 Otto Frank's card from the records of the Jewish Council in Westerbork. "Returned!" is later written on the card by a Red Cross worker. The exclamation mark indicates just how exceptional this was. Only 5,200 people return from the camps in the East.

2 Sal and Rose Deliema with Otto Frank in Amsterdam, 1967.

Sally Deliema becomes friends with Otto Frank in Auschwitz and later recalls: "Otto Frank asked me to call him papa. He knew I had nothing and I knew he had nothing. And that's why we held onto each other Papa Frank and myself... we talked about Beethoven and of course we had other things on our heads than Beethoven but we did it. And we were singing a little bit to each other and we were talking about Rembrand and all those things just to keep our minds off what

1

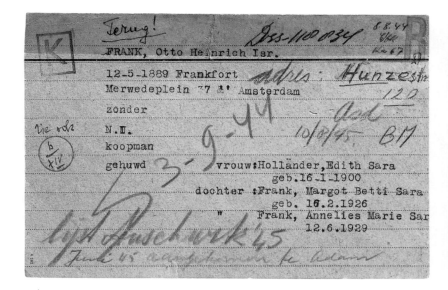

2

3

...as going on." Nevertheless, Otto gets very sick and ...ars for his life.

...The doctor came to my barrack. He said: 'Get up ...nd come to the sick-bay barrack tomorrow. I'll talk to ...e German doctor and make sure that you are ...dmitted.' That's how it went. That's how I was saved."
...Otto Frank)

...iberated prisoners standing in front of the sick-bay ...arrack in Auschwitz. The paradox is that Otto Frank ...urvives for the simple reason that he's completely ...xhausted. He therefore remains in the sick-bay barrack ...nd does not accompany the others during the evacu- ...tion. Certainly, the *SS*-guards have plans to kill the ...risoners who are left behind but they have to flee from ...e Russians and they run out of time. When Auschwitz ...s liberated Otto Frank weighs only 115 lbs.

4 In this cloth satchel, Otto Frank keeps the few things that he leaves Auschwitz with: a needle with a few threads, some pieces of paper. *"I can barely imagine normal human relationships. Here I am a beggar and that's how I also look,"* he writes to his mother from Katowice, Poland on March 18, 1945.

5 During the journey home, lasting so many months because everything is in chaos after the war, Otto makes notations in this small notebook.

6 Otto Frank's repatriation card, an important document needed for traveling. During his return trip home, Otto Frank spends a short time in the Displaced Persons Camp in Lustin, France. He arrives back in Amsterdam on June 3, 1945, more than four months after his liberation from Auschwitz.

7 On July 7, 1945, Otto Frank writes to his second cousin Milly Stanfield: *"I have to take the fact of Edith's fate but I still hope to find my children and that is at the moment all I live for...I waver between hope and fear..."* On July 21st, he writes to his mother and brothers that he has heard that Margot and Anne died in Bergen-Belsen.
"Daily I tried to speak to people about the girls. I spoke to quite a number who met them in Bergen-Belsen in Jan./Febr. but I could not trace them any further. Now I know all the truth." (Otto Frank)

"The friends here could save some photos and the diary of Anne. I had it in my hands but I couldn't read it yet." (Otto Frank)

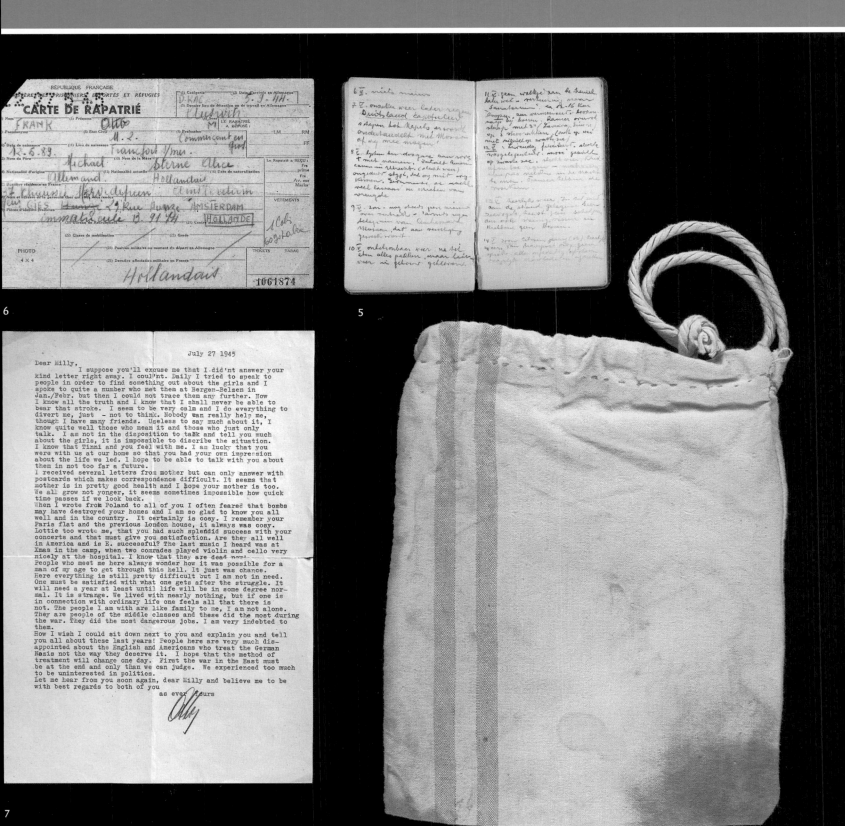

6

5

July 27 1945

Dear Milly,
I suppose you'll excuse me that I did'nt answer your kind letter right away. I coul'nt. Daily I tried to speak to people in order to find something out about the girls and I spoke to quite a number who met them at Bergen-Belzen in Jan./Febr. but then I could not trace them any further. Now I know all the truth and I know that I shall never be able to bear that stroke. I seem to be very calm and I do everything to divert me, just - not to think. Nobody can really help me, though I have many friends. Useless to say much about it, I know quite well those who mean it and those who just only talk. I am not in the disposition to talk and tell you much about the girls, it is impossible to discribe the situation. I know that Tinni and you feel with me. I am lucky that you were with us at our home so that you had your own impression about the life we led. I hope to be able to talk with you about them in not too far a future.
I received several letters from mother but can only answer with postcards which makes correspondence difficult. It seems that mother is in pretty good health and I hope your mother is too. We all grow not yonger, it seems sometimes impossible how quick time passes if we look back.
When I wrote from Poland to all of you I often feared that bombs may have destroyed your homes and I am so glad to know you all well and in the country. It certainly is cosy. I remember your Paris flat and the previous London house, it always was cosy. Lottie too wrote me, that you had such splendid success with your concerts and that must give you satisfaction. Are they all well in America and is E. successful? The last music I heard was at Xmas in the camp, when two comrades played violin and cello very nicely at the hospital. I know that they are dead now.
People who meet me here always wonder how it was possible for a man of my age to get through this hell. It just was chance. Here everything is still pretty difficult but I am not in need. One must be satisfied with what one gets after the struggle. It will need a year at least until life will be in some degree nor-mal. It is strange. We lived with nearly nothing, but if one is in connection with ordinary life one feels all that there is not. The people I am with are like family to me, I am not alone. They are people of the middle classes and these did the most during the war. They did the most dangerous jobs. I am very indebted to them.
How I wish I could sit down next to you and explain you and tell you all about these last years! People here are very much dis-appointed about the English and Americans who treat the German Nazis not the way they deserve it. I hope that the method of treatment will change one day. First the war in the East must be at the end and only than we can judge. We experienced too much to be uninterested in politics.
Let me hear from you soon again, dear Milly and believe me to be with best regards to both of you
as ever yours

7

"You've known for a long time that my greatest wish is to be a journalist and later on, a famous writer. In any case, after the war I'd like to publish a book called *The Secret Annex*."

May 11, 1944

Anne Frank's Diaries

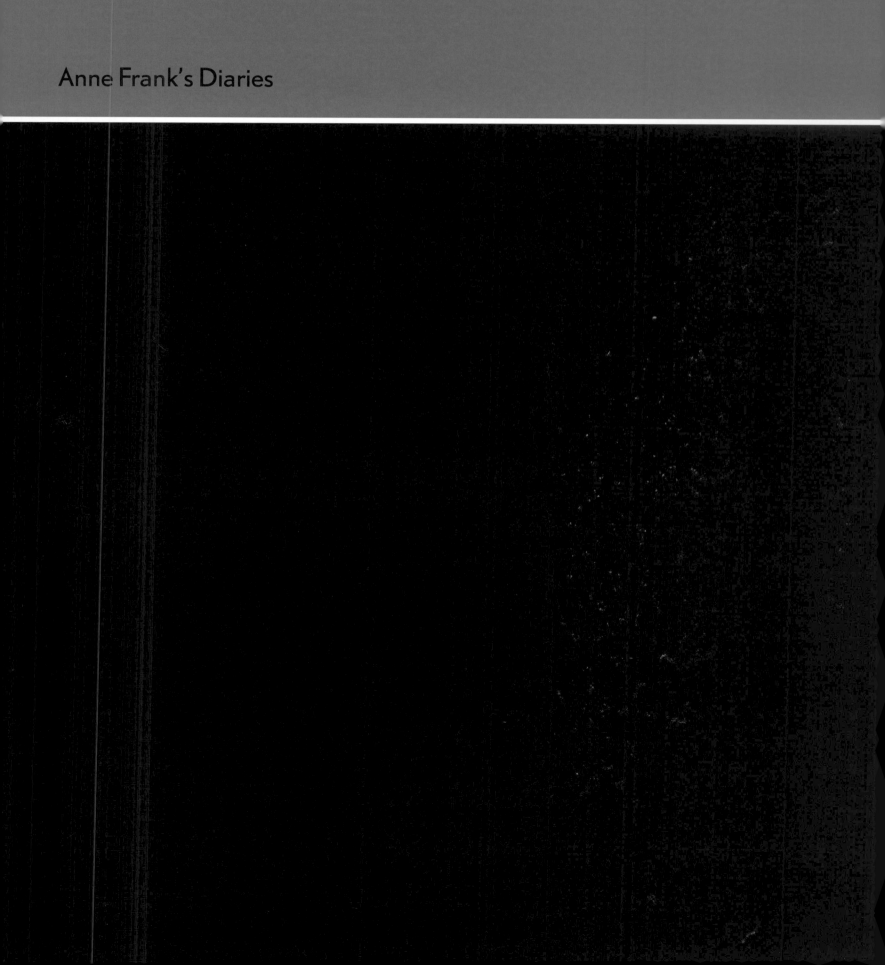

Anne Frank receives this diary on June 12, 1942, just before going into hiding. She immediately begins to use it. In the beginning, she mainly writes about her experiences at school. She also describes every pupil in her class in a few lines. It is a diary like many girls keep and have kept. Much attention is paid to boys, school and girlfriends. On the first page, she writes: *"I hope I will be able to confide everything to you, as I have never been able to confide in anyone, and I hope you will be a great source of comfort and support."* (June 12, 1942)

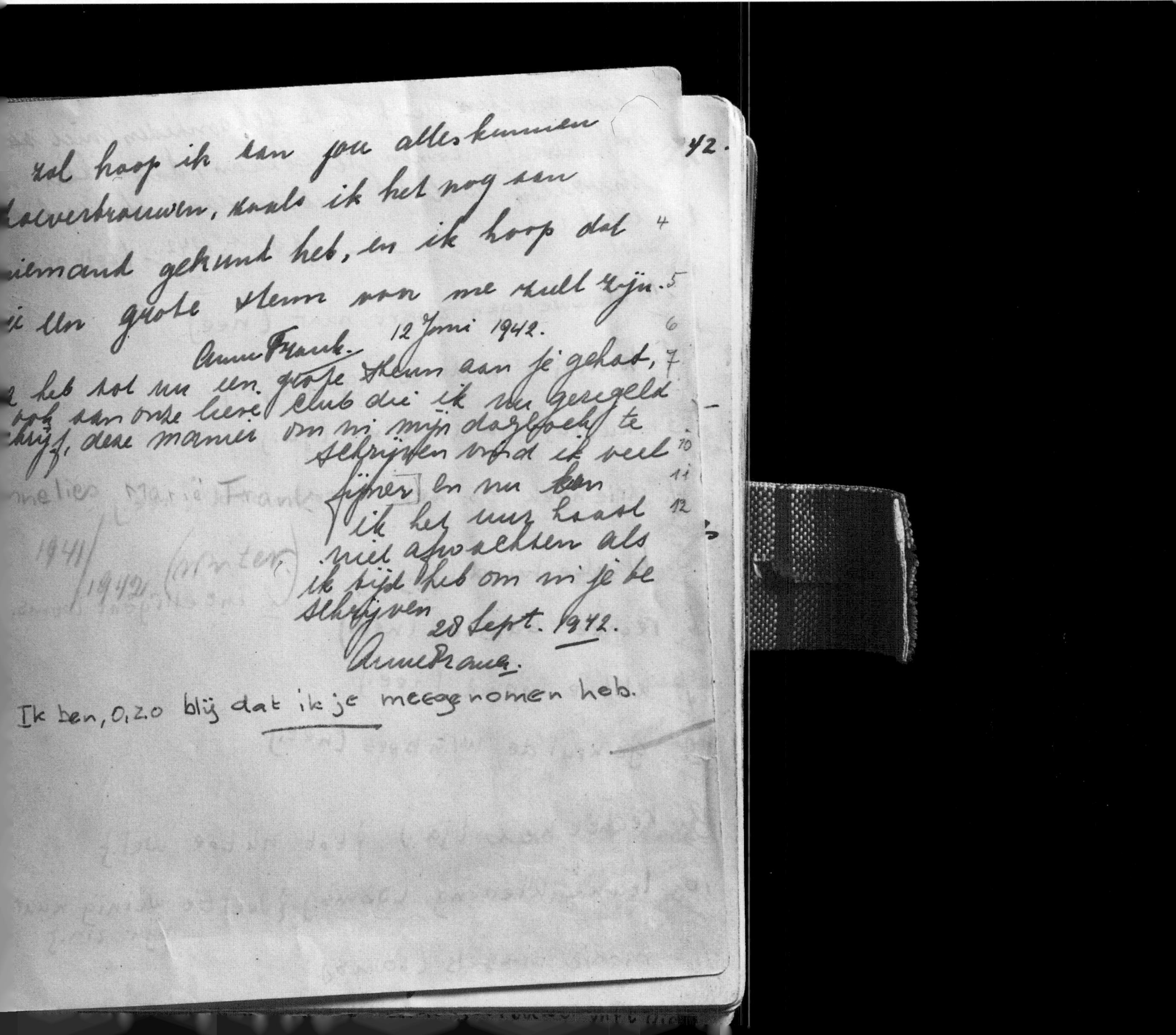

zal hoop ik aan jou alles kunnen
toevertrouwen, zaals ik het nog aan
niemand gekunt heb, en ik hoop dat
ji Un grote steun van me zull zijn.
Anne Frank. 12 Juni 1942.
ik heb tot nu un grote steun aan je gehat,
ook aan onze lieve club die ik nu geregeld
schrijf, deze manier om nu mijn dagboek te
schrijven vind ik veel
fijner en nu ben
ik het nu haast
niet afwachten als
ik tijd heb om nu je te
schrijven 28 Sept. 1942.
Anne Frank.

Ik ben, O.Z.O blij dat ik je meegenomen heb.

1941
1942 (winter)
melies Marië Frank

1 A few weeks later the Frank family has to to go into hiding, in effect, to escape persecution. Anne reads a lot during the hiding period. Every other week, Jo Kleiman brings along some girl's books for her to read. Anne is especially inspired by the popular *Joop ter Heul* books, an archetypical series of books for young girls, written by Cissy van Marxveldt. Joop ter Heul has a number of close girl friends. From that moment on, Anne addresses her diary letters to this imaginary club of friends.

"I'm enthusiastic about the Joop ter Heul *series. I've enjoyed all of Cissy van Marxveldt's books very much. I've read* The Zaniest Summer *four times, and the ludicrous situations still make me laugh."* (September 21, 1942)

2 During the hiding period Anne's writing becomes more and more insightful. The situation causes her to examine her feelings and she begins to think more and more about herself and the people around her. Anne is very self-critical, so she can candidly write about her own behavior. But she also subjects the other people in hiding to her critical analysis.

3 The diary that Anne had received for her birthday is quickly full.

4 The helpers give her bookeeping notebooks and loose sheets of paper and sometimes Margot also gives her paper so that she can keep on writing. *"Someone's been a real darling again and has torn up a chemistry exercise book for me to make a new diary, this time the someone was Margot."*

5 Anne also writes a large number of short stories in the period from July 1943 to May 1944. In the beginning these stories are primarily centered around things that happen during the hiding period. Later, she also writes a number of fairy tales and story lines for novels. *"A few weeks ago I started writing a story, something I made up from beginning to end, and I've enjoyed it so much that the products of my pen are piling up."* (August 7, 1943)

6 Beginning on August 14, 1943, Anne also copies down beautiful or interesting passages or quotations that she's read. She gets the idea for this "favorite quotes notebook" from her father. Many passages and quotations are taken classic literature (Shakespeare and Goethe), others are from novels published in the 1930's and 1940's.

1

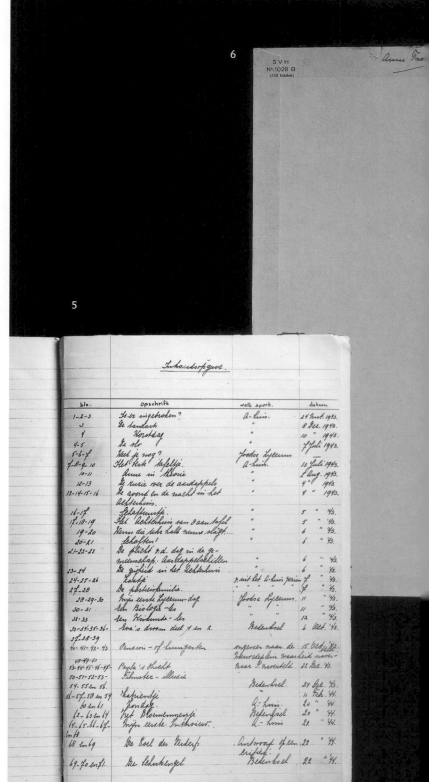

6

5

3

Achterhuis 14 Augustus 1943.
—

uitvinding van Pim!

bij de grote God nog eens aardappelen of zoete
worteltjes en dan weer binnen komen.
Aardappels eten, we voor elke maaltijd, de
beginnen bij het ontbijt, wegens gebrek aan brood,
maar aan kijk te nog, een halve gebakken.
Bij wei, denen, we binne en Hollse bonen,
aardappels, prilleins uit pakjes, borningrine
uit pakjes, bruine bonen uit pakjes.
En alles uit binne komen, niet het minst
in het brood.
't Laastde eten we altijd aardappels met
bruine, maar dat eten & we gelukkig nog,
rode bieten sla over de wegels vallen alwat ik
dot nog spreken, die maken we van wegen-
bloem niet dat vals en pref. Ne, kijn ko plezie-
rig en praai dat het rij of er sterren in je
waag liggen, maar effen!
Eens grootste attractie is het plakje leverworst
elle weeg en de jaan op droog brood. Maar
we leven nog en het is zelf best nog lekker!
je Anne M. Frank.

Maar je nog nooit een oorlog meegemaakt
hebt, Kitty en je bovendans al in je brieven toch
nog weinig van schuilen afweet, dat ik je voor
de aardigheid eens vertellen dat uur de eerste
keer dat om achter is als we weer eens naar
binnen komen.
Margot en Mijnheer v. Pels wensen zich het meest
en het bad tot foven aantoe en willen daar wel
meer dan een half uur pikkelen. Mevrouw
v. P. geel het liefst dadelijk hakselpje gaan eten.
Pij zegt, mich als t'n Charlotte, maken haar
kop koffie, Vader gaat naar fookruyts, Peter naar
de spar en in de boorcoop en ik kan van de
zaligheid niet beten, waar ik beginnen.
                    je Anne.

                            Woensdag 5 April 1944.
Liefste Kitty,
Een hele tijd! wist ik helemaal niet meer waarvoor
ik uur werk, het einde van de oorlog is zo ont-
zettend ver, zo onmenselijk sprookje-achtig en
moor. Als de oorlog in September nog niet
afgelopen is dan ga ik niet meer naar school.
Want twee jaar wil ik niet achter komen.
De dagen bestonden uit Peter, niets dan Peter,
dromen en gedachten, toldat ik Katerdagavond

1 As the hiding period progresses, writing becomes more and more important for Anne. She notes on April 5, 1945: *"When I write I can shake off all my cares. My sorrow disappears. My spirits are revived!"*

2 The other people in hiding are very curious about Anne's writings. Occasionally she reads something to the others, but only from her story book. *"I was upstairs this morning since I promised Mrs. van P. (Van Pels) I'd read her some of my stories. I began with 'Eva's Dream,' which she liked a lot, and then I read a few passages from 'The Secret Annex,' which had her in stitches. Peter also listened for a while (just the last part) and asked if I'd come to his room sometime to read more."* (February 17, 1944)

3 Anne immediately honors his request, which is also based on her desire *"to go more deeply into matters"* with Peter. She lets him read part of a story in which the leading characters talk about what God means to them.

"I decided I had to take a chance right then and there, so I got my story notebook and let him read that bit where Cady and Hans talk about God. I can't really tell what kind of impression it made on him. He said something I don't quite remember, not about whether it was good, but about the idea behind it. I told him that I just wanted to prove to him that I didn't write only amusing things. He nodded, and then left the room. We'll see if I hear anything more!" (February 17, 1944)

Left page

33.

de stoute scholieren aan en beantwoordde het grapje, met
een ander grapje, ik schreef u.l. een opstel ~~over~~ met be-
hulp van Cauta Lelenmann in rijm, en het werk duidelijk
luidt als volgt.
"Lach, lach, lach," zei juffrouw Snaterbek,
Zei wij haar kindertjes riep.
Zij kwamen, piep, piep, piep,
"Heb jij nog brood voor ons,
Voor Gerrit, Mietje en Alphons?"
"Ja zeker heb ik het al.
Ik heb het gezocht en gevonden aan wal,
Ik heb het voor jullie moeten stelen.
Hier hebben jullie het, maar eerlijk delen!"
De eendjes volgden de raad van hun niet,
En elk nam wat hem eerlijk kwam toe,
Zij riepen daarbij: fuk, fuk, fuk,"
En.. ik heb lekker het grootste stuk!"
Maar oh, daar kwam papa, de zwaan,
Op het geschreeuw, heel kwaad al van..
                              enz. enz.
Leuning las het; las het in de klas voor, nog in een paar
andere klassen en gaf zich gewonnen.
Vanaf die tijd kon ik een potje bij hem breken. Op het
gepraat sloeg hij geen acht meer en ik kreeg nooit meer
straf.
Dikwijls kiet men toch dat het een gezellige vent was.
De naam Juf. Snaterbek heb ik den aan hijzelf Leuning
te danken.

Eva's droom
deel I

"Nacht Eva, slaap lekker!"
"Van 't zelfde mams!"
Knip ging het licht uit en Eva lag even in 't donker
want toen ze aan de duisternis gewend was, zag ze
dat moeder net zo de gordijnen gesloten had, dat er
nog een hele reet open bleef, en door die reet kon Eva
net in het bekende gezicht van de maan kijken.
De maan stond zo rustig aan de hemel, hij bewoog
zich niet, hij lachte aldoor en was tegen iedereen even
vriendelijk.

Right page

1.

Ik heb veel ideeën en ben bezig ze samen te
rijmen tot één geheel. Om een overzicht te
krijgen en omdat ik anders geen lijntjes-
papier heb, schrijf ik het maar hier achterin.

Cady's leven.

1e deel: hoofdstuk I.
   Toen Cady haar ogen opende, was het eerste
wat ze zag, dat alles rondom haar wit was.
Het laatste wat ze duidelijk wist was, dat iemand
haar riep.... een auto, toen viel ze..... en toen
was alles donker. Ze voelde nu ook een stekende
pijn in haar rechterbeen en haar linkerarm en
zonder dat ze het wist kreunde ze zachtjes. Dadelijk
daarop boog zich een vriendelijk gezicht over haar
heen, dat onder een witte kap uitkeek.
"Heb je veel pijn, kleintje. Herinner je je iets van
wat er met je gebeurd is?" vroeg de zuster.
"Het is niets....."
De zuster glimlachte. Toen vervolgde Cady, moeilijk
sprekend: "ja.... een auto, ik viel.... dan niets meer!"
"Zeg me dan alleen nog even hoe je heet, dan kunnen
je ouders je opzoeken en hoeven ze niet langer in
ongerustheid te zitten!"
Cady schrok zichtbaar: "Maar.... maar, maar eh....
Meer bracht ze niet uit.

1 Anne also reads aloud a short story about a small bear who *"wants to discover the world"* to – presumably – Margot, Peter, and Bep Voskuijl.

"I have written a lovely story called 'Blurry, the Explorer, 'which pleased the three to whom I read it very much." (April 25, 1944)

2 She writes another short story entitled "Ellen, the Fairy" especially for her father. She wants to give it to him as a present for his 55th birthday. *"I've finished my story about Ellen, the fairy. I've copied it out on nice notepaper, decorated it with red ink and sewn the pages together. The whole thing looks quite pretty, but I don't know if it's enough of a birthday present. Margot and mother have both written birthday poems."* (May 9, 1944)

3 Anne is even already planning to send one of her fairy tales to a magazine for publication.

"I want to ask the magazine 'The Prince' if they'll take one of my fairytales, under a pseudonym, of course. But up to now all my fairytales have been too long, so I don't think I have much of a chance." (April 21, 1944)

De Fee.   Die

, die ik bedoel was geen gewone fee,
als zovele te vinden zijn in sprookjesland.
mijn fee was een heel bijzondere fee,
niet in haar uiterlijk en bijzonder in
manier van doen! Waarom zal nu
bragen was die fee dan zo bijzonder?
dat zij niet hier wat hielp en daar
het maakte, maar omdat zij het zich
ook had gesteld, wereld en mensen te
...en.
...zondere fee heette Ellen. Haar ouders
gestorven toen zij nog maar heel
was, maar hadden haar veel geld na-
... Ellen kon dus al als klein meisje
even wat zij behoefd en alles kopen wat
... wilde hebben. Andere kinderen,
... of elfjes houden daardoor bemind
... rijk, maar daar Ellen altijd
bijzonder was, werd zij helemaal
bemind!
zij ouder werd had zij nog steeds
...ld, en dat diende hergens anders
... om mooie dieren te kopen en
... eten.

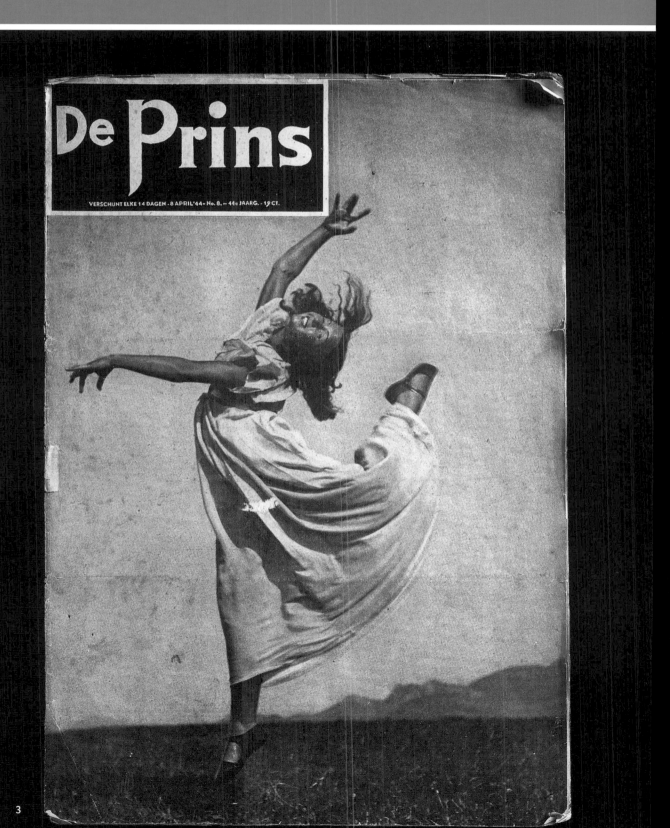

1 On March 28, 1944, the people in hiding listen to the radio broadcast of the Dutch government in exile in England. Minister Bolkestein urges listeners to save personal documents about the war. The people in hiding immediately point to Anne's diary. Anne, herself, also immediately starts to fantasize about a novel entitled "The Secret Annex". She thinks the title sounds intriguing, as if it were a detective novel. *"But, seriously, it would be quite funny ten years after the war if we Jews were to tell how we lived and what we ate and what we talked about here. Although I tell you a lot, still, even so, you only know very little of our lives"* (March 29, 1944)

2 Anne thinks more about her ambitions and what she wants to achieve with writing. She becomes more and more certain that she wants to be a journalist and writer. She is reasonably pleased with her "Achterhuis" descriptions but feels that it still hasn't been indisputably proven that she has real talent. There is still room for improvement. *"'Eva's Dream' is my best fairytale, and the odd thing is that I don't have the faintest idea where it came from. Parts of 'Cady's Life' are also good, but as a whole it's nothing special. I'm my best and harshest critic. I know what's good and what isn't."* (April 5, 1944)

3 Two months after Bolkestein's radio broadcast, Anne's ideas about "The Secret Annex" begin to take concrete form. On May 11, 1944, she writes with resolve that she wants to publish such a book after the war. *"It remains to be seen whether I'll succeed, but my diary can serve as the basis."* (May 11, 1944)

1 Sometime around May 20, 1944, Anne begins the actual work on *The Secret Annex*. In approximately ten weeks, she rewrites a large part of the original version of her diary onto loose sheets of paper. She now consistently directs all correspondence to just one imaginary friend from the earlier girls club: Kitty.

"At long last after a great deal of reflection I have started my 'Achterhuis', in my head it is as good as finished, although it won't go as quickly as that really, if it ever comes off at all." (May 20, 1944)

2 During the short period between May 20, 1944 and her arrest on August 4, 1944, Anne revises and edits her original diary. Sometimes there are small corrections in the text and sometimes she omits complete passages, for example, regarding her sexuality. An example of a text revision follows here, first the original, and then the

rewritten version: *"Believe me Kitty, if you have been shut up for 1½ years, it can indeed get to be too much for you somedays. No matter if it's unfair or ungrateful, you can't get rid of your feelings. Cycling again, dancing, flirting and what-have-you, how I would love that; if only I were free again! Sometimes I even think, will anybody understand me, will anybody overlook my ungratitude, overlook Jew or non-Jew, and just see the young girl in me who is badly in need of some rollicking fun? I don't know and I couldn't talk about it to anybody, because then I know I should cry."*
(December 24, 1943, Original Version)

"Believe me, if you have been shut up for 1½ years, it can get to be too much for you somedays. In spite of all justice and thankfulness you can't get rid of your feelings. Cycling, dancing, whistling, looking out at the world, feeling young, to know that I'm free – that's what

I long for; still I mustn't show it, because I sometimes think if all eight of us began to pity ourselves, or went about with discontented faces, where would it lead us?"
(December 24, 1943, Revised Version)

In addition to this, Anne also continues to keep her daily diary. The last loose sheet containing rewritten text is dated March 29, 1944. Up until that day, Anne makes headway in revising the original version of her diary. In ten weeks time, Anne fills an average of four or five pages per day.

4,

mogen wij weer eens de lucht ruiken?
Geloof me, Kitty, als je 1½ jaar zo opgesloten
zit, dan kan het je op sommige dagen, wel
eens teveel worden. Of het rechtvaardig of
ondankbaar is, het gevoel laat zich niet weg
cijferen.
Ook weer eens fietsen, dansen, fluiten en weet-ik-
wat-nog-meer, dat zou ik wel willen smar-
ten; als ik eerst maar weer eens vrij ben!
Ik denk zelf wel eens, zou iemand me hierin
begrijpen, zou iemand over de ondankbaarheid
heenkijken, heenkijken over Jood of niet Jood,
alleen maar in me zien de bakvis, die zo'n
behoefte heeft naar uitgelaten pret? Ik weet het
niet en ik zou er ook niet, met niemand over
kunnen spreken, want ik weet dat ik dan
ga huilen. Huilen kan zo'n verluchting brengen,
als je maar bij iemand kunt huilen en ondanks
alles, ondanks theorieën en moeiten, mis ik
elke dag en elk uur, de moeder, die me begrijpt.
En daarom, ook, denk ik bij alles wat ik doe
en wat ik schrijf, dat ik later voor mijn kinderen wil zijn; de mams, die ik me voorstel.
De mams, die niet alles zo ernstig opvat wat
er gezegd wordt, en wel ernstig opvat, wat
van me komt. Ik merk, ik kan het niet

5,

Wat de rest van me mag denken, ik
kan niet alles voor mezelf bewaren en
haal dan nog maar eens m'n begin-
woorden aan "papier is geduldig".
Als iemand net van buiten komt, met
de wind in zijn kleren en de kou op z'n
gezicht, dan zou ik wel m'n hoofd onder
de dekens willen stoppen, om niet te
denken: Wanneer is het ons weer ge-
gund lucht te ruiken." En omdat ik
m'n hoofd niet in dekens mag steken,
gen, het integendeel rechtop en flink
moet houden, komen de gedachten
toch, niet een keer, maar vele, ontel-
bare malen.
Geloof me, als je 1½ jaar opgesloten zit,
dan kan het je op sommige dagen
eens teveel worden. Of het rechtvaardig-
heid of ondankbaarheid ten spijt, ge-
voelens laten zich niet wegcijferen.
Fietsen, dansen, fluiten, de wereld
in kijken, mij jong voelen, te weten dat
ik vrij ben, daar naar ik maar en toch
mag ik het niet laten merken, want denk
eens aan als we alle 8 ons zouden
beklagen of ontevreden gezichten
zetten, maar wat dat toch weer hoe?

243
Die arme mensen, je Anne.

"I want to be useful or bring enjoyment to all people. I want to go on living even after my death! And therefore I am so grateful to God for giving me this gift of writing, of expressing all that is in me!"

April 5, 1944

The Publication of the Diary

1 Otto Frank in his office on Prinsengracht shortly after his return from Auschwitz. The tattooed number on his arm is clearly visible.

In the middle of July 1945, when Otto hears the terrible news that also both his daughters have died in the camps, Miep Gies hands him Anne's notebooks with the words: *"Here is your daughter Anne's legacy to you."*

Otto informs his family in the United States and England, as well as his mother and sister in Switzerland, about the death of Anne and Margot. In a letter he writes to his mother on August 22, 1945, he mentions Anne's diary for the first time: *"As luck would have it, Miep was able to rescue a photo album and Anne's diary. I didn't have the strength to read it."* But once he begins reading the diary, he cannot put it down.

On September 26, 1945, Otto writes to his sister, Leni Elias-Frank about Anne's diary: *"What I read in her book is so incredibly exciting that I cannot stop reading. It's impossible to explain! I haven't finished it yet and I want to before I translate fragments for you."* He writes to his mother four days later: *"I cannot put down Anne's diary. It is so unbelievably engrossing I will never give up control of the diary because there are too many things in it that nobody else should read. But I will make a selection."*

2 Otto later talks about his first reactions to reading the diary: *"I was overwhelmed by painful memories. It was a revelation for me. Before my eyes appeared a completely different Anne than the daughter that I had lost. Such profound thoughts and feelings, I had no idea at all. She had kept all those feelings to herself. Sometimes she read us funny episodes and stories but* *she never read us anything about herself. And so we never knew how intense her personal development was; and of all of us, she was the most self-critical."*

3 Otto makes a transcript of Anne's texts with his revisions. He uses, as he later explains, *"what's most important"* from the diary. He leaves out, as far as he's concerned, the uninteresting parts and personal observations that *"are nobody elses's business"*. Otto writes to Milly Stanfield about this on September 16, 1945: *"There are several things she did not see right and she would have changed her ideas. In fact she was on very good terms with her mother at the camp later. But it is a disagreeable feeling to publish things against her mother – and I have to do it. There are passages I can scrap, for instance, what she thought about my marrying Edith. It keeps my brain busy every day."* Otto shortens Anne's text and translates it into German.

1

2

his version is sent to his mother in Basel who doesn't understand Dutch.

Following the completion of the shortened version for his mother, Otto makes a new and more extensive transcript on his typewriter. This compilation is based on Anne's second and last version. Yet, here he also omits parts of the diary. Moreover, in this revised version, Otto inserts fragments that he thinks are important, taken from the original version of Anne's diary. He also adds four stories from Anne's notebook "Stories and events in the Secret Annex".

Otto has Ab Cauvern, an old friend, proofread and correct the transcript, and Ab's wife Isa, who used to work for Otto's company, types a new copy. Otto has few close friends read the corrected text. One of the readers is Dr. Kurt Baschwitz. In a letter to his daughter, he refers to it: *"It is the most shocking contemporary document that I know of, also as a piece of literature it is an amazing masterpiece. I think that it has to be published."* Otto says later, *"At first I had many doubts, but I began more and more to see that they were right."* Another friend, Dr. Werner Cahn, offers to look for a publisher. Yet, this proves to be more difficult than expected. Diverse publishers are simply not interested.

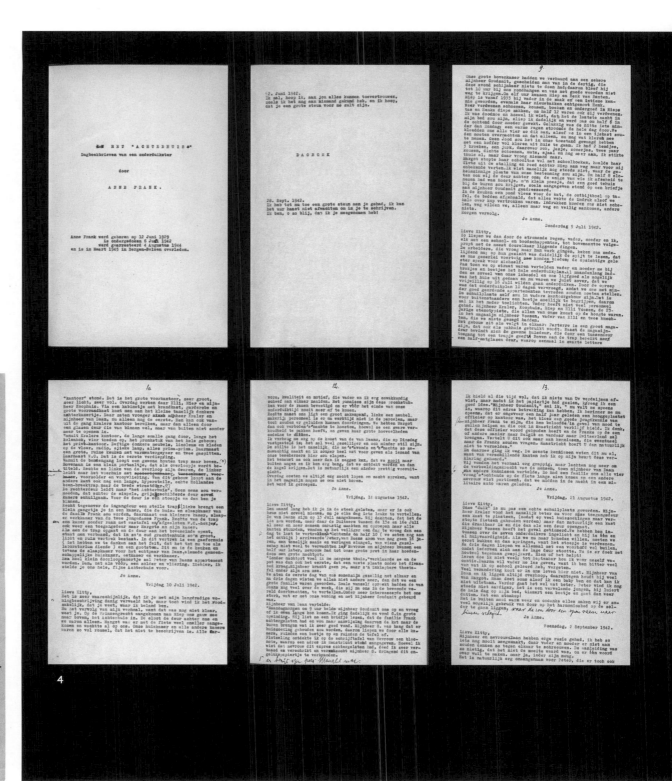

1. The manuscript is given to the historian and Dutch scholar, Dr. Annie Romein-Verschoor, who passes it on to her husband, the historian Dr. Jan Romein. Both of them are deeply impressed by the diary. Dr. Romein writes a front page article entitled *Kinderstem* or 'A Child's Voice', for the widely circulated daily Dutch newspaper *Het Parool*, formerly a Resistance newpaper. In it he concludes: *"It is clear to me that in this seemingly inconsequential child's diary, all the hideousness of fascism is embodied, more so than in all the evidence presented at Nuremberg put together."* This article attracts much attention. Also from the publishing company, Contact.

2. Pressure is applied by the director of the publishing company Contact to remove a few more passages from the text. He is of the opinion that Anne writes too freely about her sexuality. The publishing company's chief editor also makes a few changes. Noted in Otto Frank's datebook on June 25, 1947 is the word: "BOOK".

3. Anne Frank's book, *The Secret Annex: Diary Letters from June 14, 1942 to August 1, 1944*, is published on June 25, 1947 in an edition of 1,500 copies. With this, Otto Frank succeeds in fulfilling the wish of his daughter. The book is very well received in the Netherlands. The first Dutch edition is quickly sold out. In December 1947, a second edition is issued.

4. In 1946, a German translation is made of Otto's typed version by Anneliese Schütz, a journalist and acquaintance of his. She was also an acquaintance of Anne and Margot's. She actually ends up not being the most suitable person to translate Anne's text. Otto later admits that she was in fact too old to capture the youthful tone in Anne's writing. Furthermore, she sometimes makes huge blunders when translating the Dutch expressions.

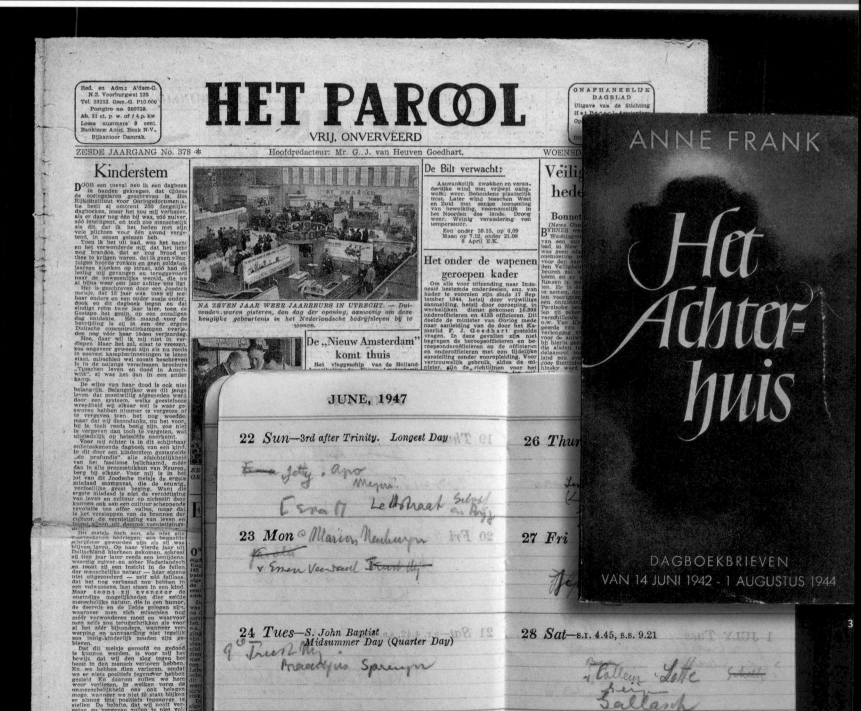

Wir begannen schnell,sie einzusammeln,aber Bohnen sind so klein
und glatt,dass sie einem immer wieder durch die Finger gleiten und
in allen Ritzen und Löchern verschwinden.Jedes Mal,wenn jetzt jemand
die Treppe heraufgeht,findet er noch Bohnen und liefert sie oben
bei Frau v.Daan ab.
      Beinahe hätte ich das wichtigste vergessen:Vater ist wieder
gesund !

      P.S. Eben kommt die Radiomeldung,dass Algier gefallen ist.
Marokko,Casablanca und Oran sind auch seit einigen Tagen in eng=
lischen Händen.Nun muss bald Tunis fallen.

                              10.November 1942.

      Liebe Kitty !

      Eine epochemachende Neuigkeit! Wir wollen einen achten
"Untertaucher" aufnehmen. Wir hatten schon oft gedacht,dass hier
noch Platz und Essen für noch jemand ist.Wir wollten nur Kraler und
Koophuis nicht noch mehr aufbürden.Als aber die Berichte von den
grausamen Juden-Verfolgungen draussen immer schlimmer wurden,hat
Vater bei den beiden Herren auf den Busch geklopft und die fanden
die Idee ausgezeichnet.
      "Die Gefahr ist dieselbe,für sieben oder für acht",sagten
sie sehr richtig.
      So weit gekommen,überlegten wir dann,welcher alleinstehende
Mensch aus unserem Bekanntenkreis gut in unsere "Taucher-Familie"
passen würde. Es war nicht schwer einen zu finden. Nachdem Vater alle
Vorschläge von v.Daan's abgewiesen hatte, jemanden aus ihrer Familie
aufzunehmen,fiel unsere Wahl auf einen bekannten Zahnarzt namens
Albert Dussel.Er steht im Ruf,ein angenehmer Mensch zu sein und
ist uns und v.Daan's sympathisch.Da Miep ihn gut kennt,kann
sie alles regeln.Wenn er kommt,muss er in meinem Zimmer schlafen
anstelle von Margot,die dann mit dem Harmonikabett ins Zimmer der
Eltern zieht.

                              12.November 1942.

      Liebe Kitty !

      Dussel war sehr glücklich,als Miep ihm sagte,dass sie ein
Versteck für ihn wüsste.Sie riet ihm,möglichst schnell zu kommen,
am liebsten übermorgen.Er hatte Bedenken,weil er seine Kartothek
noch ordnen wollte,zwei Patienten behandeln und die Rechnung fertig
machen.Diese Nachricht brachte Miep heute morgen.Wir fanden es rich=
tiger,die Sache nicht zu verzögern.Solche Vorbereitungen erfordern
Erklärungen an verschiedene Menschen,die besser gar nichts davon
wissen.Miep sollte Dussel noch mal fragen,bereits Samstag zu kommen.
Er sagte nein und kommt nun am Montag.Es ist lächerlich,dass er nicht
direkt zugegriffen hat.Wenn er auf der Strasse mitgenommen wird,
kann er die Kartothek auch nicht mehr ordnen und weder Kasse machen noch
die Patienten behandeln.Ich finde es falsch von Vater,dass er sich
umkriegen liess ! Sonst nichts Neues.

                              17.November 1942.

      Liebe Kitty !

      Dussel ist hier.Es ist alles gut gegangen.Miep hatte ihn vor
das Hauptpostamt bestellt.Er war pünktlich.Herr Koophuis,der ihn
kannte,ging hin und sagte ihm,dass der Herr - zu dem er angeblich
sollte - etwas später käme und Dussel sollte inzwischen bei Miep
im Büro warten.Koophuis fuhr mit der Elektrischen zurück,Dussel
ging zu Fuss und war um halb zwölf im Büro.Er musste den Mantel
ausziehen,damit man den Stern nicht sah und bei Koophuis im Privat-
Büro warten,bis die Aufräumefrau weg war.Diesen Grund wusste er
natürlich nicht.Dann ging Miep mit Dussel unter dem Vorwand,dass
eine Besprechung im Büro sein würde,in die obere Etage.Vor den Augen
des sprachlosen Mannes öffnete sie die Drehtür und beide schlüpf=
ten hinein.Wir waren oben bei v.Daan's versammelt,um den neuen
Genossen mit Kaffee und Cognac zu begrüssen.Inzwischen hatte Miep
ihn in unser Wohnzimmer gebracht.Er erkannte sofort unsere Möbel,
kam aber nicht auf den Gedanken,uns so nahe zu suchen.Als Miep es
ihm erzählte,konnte er es nicht fassen.Sie liess ihm auch keine Zeit
dazu,sondern brachte ihn nach oben.Da fiel Dussel mal erst auf einen
Stuhl,starrte uns alle der Reihe nach an und wollte seinen Augen nicht
trauen.Dann begann er zu stottern:" Aber..nein..aber sind Sie denn
nicht in Belgien ? Ist der Offizier nicht gekommen ? Das Auto ?
Ist die Flucht nicht geglückt...? "
      Nun erzählten wir ihm alles,dass wir selbst das Märchen ver-
breitet hatten von dem Offizier und dem Auto,um die Menschen und
besonders die Deutschen,wenn sie nach uns suchen würden,irre zu
führen.Dussel war sprachlos über so viel Erfindungsgeist und blieb
erstaunte noch mehr,als er dann unseren gut ausgeklügelten,fein
angelegten Schlupfwinkel näher beschnüffelte.Wir assen zusammen,dann
ruhte er ein bischen,trank Tee mit uns und ordnete dann seine Habselig-
keiten,die Miep schon vorher mitgebracht hatte.Er fühlte sich schnell
zu Haus,besonders nachdem ihm die Hausordnung der Untertaucher
(Entwurf v.Daan) überreicht worden war.

          Prospekt und Leitfaden vom Hinterhaus

      Stiftung,eigens errichtet zum provisorischen Aufenthalt für
Juden und ihresgleichen.

          Während des ganzen Jahres geöffnet

      Schöne,ruhige,w a l d freie Umgebung im Herzen von Amsterdam.
Zu erreichen mit Linien 13 und 17,mit Auto und Fahrrad,für
diejenigen,denen die Deutschen den Gebrauch jeglicher Fahr=
gelegenheit verboten haben,jedoch erreichbar auch zu Fuss.

          Wohnungsmiete

Gratis.

          Fettfreie Diätküche

          Fliessendes Wasser

Im Badezimmer(leider ohne Bad) und verschiedentlich an Aussen=
mauern und Wänden.

          Geräumiges Magazin für Güter aller Art

      Eigene Radiozentrale   mit direktem Anschluss nach
London,New York,Tel Aviv und vielen anderen Stationen.
Der Apparat steht den Bewohnern ab 6 Uhr abends zur
                                        Verfügung.

1 Otto Frank is eager to have the diary published in Germany as well. He later says about this: *"Generally, I waited until publishers in other countries contacted me, but one country I did try: Germany. I thought they should read it."* However, finding a German publisher remains a problem. It isn't until 1950 – when the Dutch edition is already in its sixth printing – that a publisher is finally found. The German edition is issued in a printing of 4,500 copies. Sales are modest. That same year, Anne's diary is also published in France.

2 In the United States the manuscript is initially rejected by a dozen or so publishers: *"I do not believe that there will be enough interest in the subject in this country to sell enough copies to make publication over here a profitable business,"* is written for example by a New York publisher. Finally in 1952, *The Diary of a Young Girl* is published in both the United States and England. The book appears in the United States in a modest printing of 5,000 copies. But following a celebrated review in *The New York Times*, a second printing of 15,000 copies is issued, and a few days later even a third printing of 45,000 copies.

3 In the years that follow, translations are published in countries such as: Japan, East Germany, Switzerland, Italy, Denmark, Sweden, Norway, Finland, Iceland, Spain, Argentina, Mexico, Uruguay, Portugal, Brazil, Greece, Turkey, Hungary, Poland, Rumania, the Soviet Union, Czechoslovakia, Yugoslavia, Israel, India, South Korea, and Thailand. The book has presently been translated into approximately 60 languages. The Japanese edition, published in 1952, is enthusiastically received. The sales figures are spectacular. Within one year, 100,000 Japanese copies are sold.

4 Otto receives more and more reactions from readers throughout the world. The Dutch Rabbi David Soetendorp recalls: *"There he sat at the dining room table, full of stories about how the diary had inspired children in faraway countries."* Otto Frank receives tens-of-thousands of letters from youngsters. All during those years, up until his death on August 19, 1980, he devotes a few hours a day to answering these letters together with his second wife Fritzi Frank-Markovits. In 1979, the year before he dies, he writes: *"I have received many thousands of letters. Young people especially always want to know how these terrible things could ever have happened. I answer them as well as I can. And then at the end, I often finish by saying: 'I hope that Anne's book will have an effect on the rest of your life so that insofar as it is possible in your own circumstances, you will work for unity and peace.'"*

4

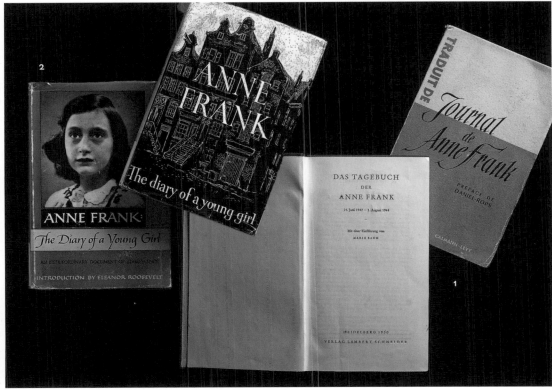

1 In the United States, preparations for a stage play based on Anne's diary begin in 1953. In the photograph (from left to right): Jo Kleiman, Mrs. Frank-Markovits, the couple Hackett-Goodrich (the creators of the stage adaption), Otto Frank next to Garson Kanin, the play's director. The stage adaption strays from the book in many aspects. Hitler and National Socialism are relegated to the background, just like the Jewish identity of Anne and the other people in hiding. To serve the dramatic line, some of the characters are portrayed only negatively, especially Fritz Pfeffer and Hermann van Pels. Still, Otto feels that the essence of the diary has been left sufficiently intact and he agrees to the production.

2 The premiere of the play takes place on October 5, 1955, at the Cort Theatre in New York City. Otto Frank is not present and in a letter he apologizes to the actors:

"You will all realize that for me this play is a part of my life, and the idea that my wife and children as well as I will be presented on the stage is a painful one to me. Therefore it is impossible for me to come and see it. I assure you that my thoughts are with everyone of you." The play is critically acclaimed in the reviews and becomes a huge success on Broadway running for 717 performances. The actors, the Hacketts and the director receive a number of important theatrical awards.

3 Queen Juliana and Prince Bernhard with Rob de Vries who portrays Otto in the first Dutch staging off the Diary. The Dutch première takes place on November 27, 1956 in the presence of the Royal Couple. The European première takes place in Sweden, Germany follows. The production makes a huge impression in Germany and attracts two million theatergoers. Following the performance there is often complete

silence in the audience, lasting several minutes. Many theater companies throughout Europe and elsewhere in the world include the play in their repertoire. Since then, the play has been performed throughout the world on innumerable occasions. In 1995, the play is partially revised by Wendy Kesselman. The historical context and the character development of Anne receiv[e] more attention, along with the fact that it revolves around Jews.

4 Shooting of the feature film "The Diary of Anne Frank" begins in 1958. The director is George Stevens The American cover girl Millie Perkins portrays Anne Frank. The Secret Annex is copied in detail and reconstructed on a set in Beverly Hills. The film is well received, earning it three Oscars that year. Yet, it is no[t] a box-office success. However, all this attention results once again in renewed worldwide interest for the boo[k]

1

2

3

5

or many people, Millie Perkins remains *the* Anne Frank. Her photograph adorns the cover of the American edition of the diary for many years. During the shooting of the film, Millie is still quite young and doesn't know very much about the historical context. The actress Shelley Winters, who plays the role of Mrs. van Pels, sympathizes with Millie. *"Millie was very worried because she knew so little about Jewish traditions or history, so I took her under my wing and tried to help her as much as possible."* Shelley Winters receives the Oscar for her role in the film. She later gives it to the Anne Frank House in Amsterdam.

In 1957, 263 Prinsengracht, the location of the hiding place, is threatened with demolition. This plan is thwarted thanks to the initiative of a few of Amsterdam's residents. The Anne Frank House organization is founded and they purchase the building. Otto Frank is appointed to the Board of Trustees. After the restoration of the building, the Secret Annex opens as a museum on May 3, 1960. This photograph of Otto Frank is taken in the attic of the Annex a few hours before the opening. Yet, Otto Frank wants to do more than just open the Secret Annex to the public. He establishes his own educational foundation, enabling youngsters from all over the world to come in contact with each other.

6

© Arnold Newman

1 The diary achieves international critical acclaim. Anne's diary is a moving testimony against the evil of National Socialism. For millions of people this book is their first encounter with the Holocaust. This leads neo-Nazis to claim that the book is a fake. As early as 1957, publications containing these sorts of allegations start appearing. Neo-Nazis also deny that the Holocaust ever occurred. They hope, in this way, to rid National Socialism of its criminal character and present it as a respectable political movement.

2 Sculpture of Anne defaced by a swastika in Utrecht (the Netherlands), 1983. Neo-Nazis attack Anne Frank's image and the diary – not only in their brochures and pamphlets.

The Internet offers new, unprecedented possibilities for neo-Nazis. This easily accessible international computer network contains a number of websites where the Holocaust is denied and Anne's diary is called a hoax. Using this technology, neo-Nazis are able to reach a new target group: countless youngsters throughout the world. Legal measures to keep these messages off the Internet hardly exist.

3 Otto Frank also devotes part of his time to court cases against neo-Nazis who claim that the diary is a forgery. He wins each and every court case but it is extremely tiring to continually have to confront these neo-Nazis. After Otto's death in 1980, the Anne Frank House and the Anne Frank Fund in Basel (Switzerland) take on the task of defending the diary against neo-Nazi attacks.

4 After his death in 1980, Otto Frank leaves the notebooks of his daughter to the Dutch State, which arranges a scientific examination of the writings. An important aspect of the study is the graphological analysis of Anne's handwriting, which proves without a doubt that the diary is authentic. The Netherlands Institute for War Documentation (*NIOD*) decides to publish the results of this investigation, along with almost all the diary notes of Anne Frank.

5 In the *Critical Edition* published by the Netherlands Institute for War Documentation a few passages are also omitted. Part of the text where Anne writes about her parents is left out at the explicit request of the family. A number of other lines are also omitted at the special request of those directly concerned. Certain names are replaced with fictitious initials. Furthermore, in 1998, it also appears that a former employee of the Anne Frank House is in possession of five unknown pages of text. These pages had always

1

3

2

een withheld by Otto because they reveal something
bout a previous love of his, and about his relationship
ith his wife, Edith.

The diary of Anne Frank has been read by millions of people throughout the world, making it the most translated Dutch book of all time. Anne Frank appeals to people from all sorts of cultures and lifestyles. Obviously there are elements in the diary that are universally recognizable by young and old.

1 Anne Frank by Mari Andriessen. This statue is located next to the *Westerkerk* (an historical Amsterdam church) only 300 feet from the Anne Frank House.

"One single Anne Frank moves us more than the countless others who suffered just as she did but whose faces have remained in the shadows. Perhaps it is better that way; if we were capable of taking in all the suffering of all those people, we would not be able to live." (Primo Levi, writer and survivor of Auschwitz)

2 Stamps from the Netherlands, Germany and Israel. Various countries have issued stamps with Anne's image.

"Some of us read Anne Frank's diary on Robben Island and derived much encouragement from it." (Nelson Mandela, president of South Africa, 1994)

3 A quilt hanging on the wall, made by women in Chile and donated to the Anne Frank House. The Anne Frank House regularly receives letters and creative work from people all over the world.

"One cannot help but be impressed with the astounding self-criticism and literary insight the barely fifteen-year-old Anne brought to bear upon the revision of her original text, omitting whole sections, reshuffling others, and adding supplementary information so as to create a more interesting and readable text. It is a shame that even now she is hardly taken seriously as a writer." (Laureen Nussbaum, professor of Literature)

4 Innumerable pamplets and books have been published about Anne Frank and her diary.

"Of the multitude who throughout history have spoken for human dignity in times of great suffering and loss, no voice is more compelling than that of Anne Frank." (John F. Kennedy, president of the United States, 1961)

5 A lithograph by Marc Chagall. Many famous artists have been inspired by Anne's text.

"The content of Anne Frank's legacy is still very much alive and it can address us fully, especially at a time when the map of the world is changing and dark

1

2

...assions are awakening within people." (Vaclav Havel, ...riter and president of the Czech Republic, 1994)

...hroughout the world, schools and streets have been ...amed after Anne Frank.

..."What is important about The Diary of Anne Frank is ...hat it demonstrates, on a level that anyone can relate ...o, the immense tragedy of the Holocaust, the waste ...f human lives and talent, and the price that was paid ...ecause free people did not act in time to to suppress ...otalitarian movements." (Yehuda Lev, philosopher ...nd writer)

3

6

5

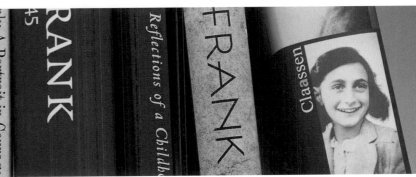

4

"Concerning the front part of the house, I would, if it's at all possible, choose for restoration, because I would also like the situation in that part of the house to remain the way Anne described it in her diary. Yet, for the time being we do not have to worry about this."

Otto Frank, June 23, 1957

The Anne Frank House

"The Secret Annex's fame is derived from a relatively short period in its existence. The building has a long and complicated history of usage, typical for Amsterdam. The building itself is a story. From the outside no one could imagine the internal layout and therefore it was suitable as a hiding place." (Engineer, Professor C.L. Temminck Groll Ph.D., advisor restoration project)

The building at 263 Prinsengracht that houses the Anne Frank House was constructed in 1635. It was one of the many mercantile houses built alongside the canal. In the 17th century the transport of raw materials and merchandise is primarily done by water. Everybody wants a building by a canal to facilitate loading in-and-out of the (ware)houses onto boats. The scarce property fronting the canal is expensive, so the houses that are built are very narrow. To still obtain the needed space, people build far into the gardens out back. For the sake of obtaining a good degree of light, people often split the building into two sections – a front part of the house and a back part, or annex. The 17th-century center of Amsterdam with its ringed canals is spaciously laid out and the gardens are deep. In the garden diagonally behind the Anne Frank House the chestnut tree has already been flourishing for more than 150 years. The canal-side houses # 263 and # 265 Prinsengracht are built at the same time. In 1739, # 263 undergoes a major renovation. A new and larger annex is built to replace the old annex in back. Down through the centuries, the building has many inhabitants and is used not only as a residence, but as a factory or place of business. Otto Frank's trading firm rents the building in 1940. Two years later the hiding period described in Anne's diary begins and this results in the house becoming world famous.

1 The third building on the left is 263 Prinsengracht, around 1956.

2 The Secret Annex and the old chestnut tree in the garden are clearly visible in the middle of the photograph, around 1950.

1

After the people in hiding are arrested, the moving company Puls removes the furniture from the Secret Annex by order of the German occupation authorities. The helpers keep the business in the front part of the house going. The rooms of the annex remain empty. After the war (in 1953) the firm Opekta, now jointly managed by Jo Kleiman and Otto Frank, purchases the building. The building is in poor condition, the walls are full of cracks and the building's foundation is weak. The equally small, sagging, and neglected buildings on the corner of the Prinsengracht and Westermarkt are bought up between 1950 and 1953 by the Berghaus Firm. *"This Firm also wanted to buy our house,"* writes Otto Frank about 1960. *"Berghaus had plans to demolish the houses and build a large office building in their place. This created a large problem for us, because we really didn't want to lose the house."* Still, because the estimated costs to repair the building

were so high and partially unforseeable, neither Otto nor the firm Opekta had enough money available. *"With a heavy heart I had to agree to sell the house to Berghaus,"* writes Otto Frank. On April 6, 1954 the sale is concluded. Protests ensue.

"We really didn't want to lose the house." (Otto Frank)

"How could people better honor the memory of Anne Frank than by saving this house, which is forever connected to Amsterdam's darkest years of occupation in terms of both literature and history." (Amsterdam Historical Society *Amstelodamum* to the Municipality of Amsterdam, 1956)

1 "Anne Frank's 'Secret Annex' is going to be torn down," reports the daily newspaper *De Tijd* on December 11, 1954 with sadness.

2 Otto Frank, the couple Frances Goodrich and Albert Hackett, and director Garson Kanin in Anne's room, December 1954. At that time, the Hacketts are adapting Anne Frank's diary for the stage. They leave for Amsterdam on December 6, 1954, so writes Frances Hackett-Goodrich in her own diary. Otto Frank himsel shows them around the house. The director has the photographer, Maria Austria, document all the details of the hiding place: doorknobs, stairs, the kitchen counter, heater, and window.

3 In 1956, the building at 263 has been vacant for some time.

Anne Frank's „Achterhuis" wordt afgebroken

Plaats waar wereldberoemd dagboek werd geschreven

Drie titelbladen van het boek van de jeugdige Anne Frank, dat in vijftien talen werd vertaald.

(Van onze verslaggever).

„Vader, moeder en Margot kunnen nóg steeds niet aan het geluid van de Westertorenklok wennen, die om het kwartier zegt hoe laat het is". Zo begon Anne Frank weer een nieuwe dag

de omgeving van meisje tot vrouw groeide, is in Nederland minder bekend dan in het buitenland. Het meisje begon haar dagboek op 12 Juni 1942, de dag dat zij dertien jaar werd. Zij schreef tot 1 Augustus 1944 alles wat in het achterhuis van het pand op de Prinsengracht gebeurde op. Haar visie was nog

Toen de Duitsers haar en haar noten, onder wie haar vader, moeder, zuster, meenamen, bleven die geschreven kladschriften achter. Frank keerde na de oorlog weer las voor het eerst het dagboek van dochter. Hij las alles wat er in derduikperiode was voorgevallen alles wat zich in die rijpende meisjeziel had afgespeeld. Zelf schreef Frank van haar dagboek: „Ik zal ik aan jou alles kunnen toevertrouwen zoals ik het nog nooit aan iemand kund heb en ik hoop dat je een grote steun voor me zult zijn".

Sinds 1947 is het boek in vele talen verschenen. Millioenen mensen namen kennis van de lotgevallen in het Achterhuis op de Prinsengracht. Op universiteiten van Amerika en Engeland gebruiken de studenten in de psychologie het als studieboek. Bijna dagelijks ontvangt de heer Frank brieven van diep ontroerde mensen uit alle werelddelen. Talloze buitenlandse bezoekers zijn de trap van het grachtenhuis opgegaan en hebben gezien waar Anne Frank leefde en groter werd. De castanjeboom achter in de tuin, de filmsterrenfoto's die Anne aan de wand had geplakt, alles waarmee de wereld door het boek vertrouwd is geraakt. Streepjes op het behang duiden aan hoe groot Anne werd en de kast met ordners die de toegang naar het achterhuis verbergt.

Binnenkort verschijnen de geschiedenissen uit het „Achterhuis" op de New-Yorkse toneelplanken. Binnenkort ook zal men aanvangen met de sloping van het „Achterhuis".

In het vervolg zullen de vele vreemdelingen en de schaarse Amsterdammers tevergeefs komen kijken naar het boek blijft.

2

3

The play "The Diary of Anne Frank" premieres in the Netherlands on November 27, 1956. The diary and the hiding place become more and more famous. Jo Kleiman receives a key from the Berghaus Firm to show the Secret Annex to people who are interested in seeing it. More and more people voice their opinion to stop the planned demolition. In January 1957, the Amsterdam City Council offers Berghaus an alternative location. The impending demolition is averted. The Anne Frank House organization is founded on May 3, 1957. This organization has as its goal *"the restoration and, if necessary, renovation of 263 Prinsengracht and especially the preservation of the attached annex, as well as the propagation of the ideals, left as a legacy to the world, in the diary of Anne Frank,"* as stated in its statutes. Otto Frank, who then lives in Switzerland, is present at the founding. Jo Kleiman represents him on the Board of Trustees. The other founders and initial

Board members are Truus Wijsmuller-Meijer, a former member of the Resistance; the concentration camp survivor and publisher, Floris Bakels; the notary, Jacob van Hasselt; the director of KLM, Herman Heldring; and the secretary of the *Bond Heemschut* (Landmark Preservation), Ton Koot. In October 1957, The Berghaus firm officially presents the building as a gift to the Anne Frank House organization.

"On the day of the premiere I visited the building with the actors again. When we were in Van Pels' room, we heard a loud banging on the door downstairs. It sounded menacing and made them understand even more the fears which ruled the lives of the people in hiding." (Jo Kleiman, December 2, 1956)

"After the Anne Frank House was restored, they asked me if the rooms should be furnished again.

But I answered: 'No!'. During the war everything was taken away and I want to leave it like that. But after the house was opened to the public, people said they felt that the rooms were very spacious. I answered that they were getting a wrong impression and said: 'You mustn't forget the unbearable tension that was constantly present.'" (Otto Frank, May 24, 1962)

1 Otto Frank with Truus Wijsmuller-Meijer, on July 19, 1957, in front of the house on the Prinsengracht, just after publically announcing the acceptance of the building as a gift.

2 In the 1950's, Jo Kleiman takes many visitors through the house.

3 The Amsterdam artist Anton Witsel making sketches of the Secret Annex, April 1958. He protests against the

1

2

anned demolition of the neighboring house, # 265
rinsengracht. This demolition would have seriously
amaged the foundation of the Anne Frank House,
erhaps leading to its collapse. The building at # 265
as also saved and is now a part of the museum.

During the restoration of the Secret Annex carried out in 1958 and 1959, the Annex is preserved in its original state when this is possible. On May 3, 1960, the house is officially opened to the pulic. Otto Frank's wish to also keep the front part of the house in it's authentic state could unfortunately not be combined with his objective to make the Anne Frank House into an international meeting place for youngsters. For that purpose, the rooms in the front part of the house, the former warehouse, and the spice grinding room are rebuilt into a lecture hall. The former offices on the second floor and the old storerooms on the third floor are replaced by spaces for exhibitions and documentation. The adjoining building contains meeting rooms and offices. The old buildings on the corner are demolished. The city builds a student dormitory on this piece of property. During the summer, young conference participants reside there. Otto Frank is a regular visitor to these conferences in the Anne Frank House, which address a diversity of topics like: the relationship between Judaism and Christianity, discrimination, prejudice and war. For visitors, scale models depicting the situation in the house during the hiding period are placed on exhibit in the Secret Annex. Visits become so numerous (about 180,000 visitors in 1970) that a structural rebuilding of the house is necessary. In the 1970's exhibitions are mounted about the Jewish persecution between 1933 and 1945 and on contemporary human rights violations. The first traveling exhibition about anti-Semitism in the early 1980's is followed in 1985 with "Anne Frank in the World, 1929-1945". All over the world, this traveling exhibition attracts many visitors. Educational work related to Anne Frank, anti-Semitism, racism and prejudice is extended – nationally and internationally.

1 Opening of the Anne Frank House, May 3, 1960. To the left Otto Frank, on the right Amsterdam's Mayor Van Hall.

2 Otto and Fritzi Frank surrounded by participants attending an international youth conference in the Anne Frank House, May 1969.

3 The student dormitory at the corner of the Prinsengracht and Westermarkt. During the summer, the students vacate their rooms and the building provides housing for participants attending the youth conferences.

1

3

2

By the early 1990s, it appears that expansion of the museum is necessary to better receive and inform the increasing number of visitors about the conditions in which Anne Frank's diary was written. In November 1993, the City of Amsterdam gives the go ahead for the project "Preservation and the Future of the Anne Frank House". During extensive rebuilding activities that last until the summer of 1999, the Secret Annex remains open to visitors. A new building, designed by the architectural firm Benthem Crouwel, is constructed on the site of the former student housing. The neighboring building at # 265 Prinsengracht is renovated. As a result of the reconstruction, the front part of the house at # 263 Prinsengracht, where the hiding place was located, is largely returned to the atmosphere and style of the hiding period. Here is where the helpers worked and where the people in hiding also came outside of working hours. For this reconstruction,

photographs taken by Maria Austria (in 1957) provided much to go by, just like the floorplans from 1957. The restoration is carried out by the architectural firm Verlaan and Bouwstra, advised by engineer, Professor Temminck Groll, Ph.D. The interior designer Marijke van der Wijst works on the museum's design and layout and is also involved in the restoration of the house. Preservation activities are conducted on the original interior of the Secret Annex. The picture wall in Anne Frank's room as well as other pieces of original wallpaper, with the penciled growth measurements and the map of Normandy, are given a protective covering. On a few occassions something is restored to exactly how it was during the hiding period. The map of Belgium is once again hanging above the original movable bookcase that hides the Secret Annex. The former color of the woodwork, determined by color testing, is applied anew. The windows are blacked-out

again. "The preservation of the Secret Annex is a sum total of details," states Professor Temminck Groll, "doorhandles, light switches, curtains, lamps, wallpaper, and floor covering. The entire atmosphere of the building at 263 Prinsengracht has become more somber. The old colors in the Secret Annex served as the sampler for the front part of the house. So here there is also more of a feeling of the 1940's; as it is now we almost expect to see the people in hiding wandering through the house on Sundays and outside of weekly working hours!"

1 Scale-model of the interior of the Secret Annex made in 1961 by J. Weiss, on the right, using details provided by Otto Frank. In addition to the photographs made by Maria Austria and the floor plans, also the scale-models were used as a source of information for the restoration done in the 1990's.

1

he reconstruction of the floor that housed the
fices, 1996.

he *Instituut Collectie Nederland**examining the
cture wall in Anne's room in connection with the
eservation, April 1999. The pieces of wallpaper hung
ith pictures are original. The other walls in the Secret
nnex are papered once again with a replica of this
allpaper, made by Rath & Doodeheefver. (* A national
stitute, which provides advise to museums and does
search for specific projects, in addition to other
lated activities.)

Restoration and the design and layout of a museum
o hand in hand. It is important to clearly show what
authentic and what has been added. For this reason
e have clearly indicated all the breakthroughs
etween the buildings that were not originally present.

Both in the front part of the house and the Secret
Annex, the space plays an essential role in enabling
viewers to be transported back in time to the hiding
period. The quotations from Anne Frank's diary
provide further information about the rooms and the
objects." (Marijke van der Wijst, Museum Designer)

"In the new building of the Anne Frank House one
is struck by the transparent and open atmosphere,
and that is also the intention. The typical Amsterdam
design that divides a house into a front part and a
back annex with a courtyard in the middle to catch
the daylight has been echoed in this new building.
The visitor, who has just come face to face with the
past, can catch his or her breath here. The spacious
exhibition room is suitable for the contemporary
themes that the Anne Frank House wants to address."
(Mels Crouwel, architect new building)

256

"I see the world gradually being turned into a wasteland, I hear the ever approaching thunder, which will destroy us too, I feel the suffering of millions of people and yet, if I look up into the heavens, I somehow feel that this will come right again, that also this savagery will stop, that there will be peace and tranquility in the world once again. Until that time, I must hold onto my ideals. Perhaps the day will come when I'll still be able to realize them." (July 15, 1944)

Appendix

Bibliography

Frank, Anne
Het Achterhuis. Dagboekbrieven 14 juni 1942 –
1 augustus 1944, Bert Bakker, Amsterdam, 1991
Frank, Anne
De Dagboeken van Anne Frank, Nederlands
Instituut voor Oorlogsdocumentatie, Bert Bakker,
1986
Frank, Anne
Verhaaltjes en gebeurtenissen uit het Achterhuis,
Bert Bakker, Amsterdam, 1986

Barnouw, David
Anne Frank voor beginners en gevorderden,
Sdu, Den Haag, 1998
Benz, Wolfgang, Hermann Graml en
Hermann Weiß
Enzyklopädie des Nationalsozialismus,
Deutscher Taschenbuch Verlag, München, 1998
Benz, Wolfgang (hrsg)
Dimension des Völkermords, R.Oldenbourg
Verlag, München, 1991
Czech, Danuta
Kalendarium der Ereignisse im Konzentrations-
lager Auschwitz-Birkenau 1939 - 1945, Rowohlt,
1989
Gies, Miep en Leslie Anne Gold
Herinneringen aan Anne Frank, Bert Bakker,
Amsterdam, 1987
Jäckel, Eberhard, Peter Longerich en
Julius H. Schoeps (hrsg)
Enzyklopedie des Holocaust, Argon, 1993
Kolb, Eberhard
Bergen-Belsen. Vom Aufenthaltslager zum
Konzentrationslager 1943 - 1945, Sammlung
Vandenhoeck, 1988
Lee, Carol Ann
Anne Frank 1929 – 1945, Pluk de rozen en vergeet
mij niet, Balans, Amsterdam, 1998
Levi, Primo
De verdronkenen en de gereddenen, Meulenhoff,
Amsterdam, 1986
Lindwer, Willy
De laatste zeven maanden, Gooi en Sticht, 1988
Maarssen, Jacqueline van
Anne en Jopie, Balans, Amsterdam, 1990
Müller, Melissa
Anne Frank – de biografie, Bert Bakker,
Amsterdam, 1998
Shapiro, Eda en Kardonne, Rick
Victor Kugler – The Man Who Hid Anne Frank,
His memoirs in his own words, 1996
Schnabel, Ernst
Spur eines Kindes, Fischer Taschenbuch Verlag,
Frankfurt am Main, 1958
Steen, Jürgen en Wolf von Wolzogen
Anne aus Frankfurt, Historisches Museum,
Frankfurt am Main, 1994
Winter-Levy, Rosa de
Aan de gaskamer ontsnapt, Misset, Doetinchem,
1945
Anne Frank Stichting
Anne Frank 1929 - 1979, Verlag Lambert Schneider,
Heidelberg, 1979

Quotation Index

John F. Kennedy, 'Kennedy, Praising Anne Frank,
Warns of New Nazi-Like Peril' in: The New York
Times, 20 September 1961
Vaclav Havel at the opening of the exhibition
'De wereld van Anne Frank 1929-1945' in Prague
(Czech Republic), 14 June 1994
Yehuda Lev, 'Revisiting our Annexes' in:
The Jewish Journal of Los Angeles, 31 March 1995
Otto Frank in a letter to Jo Kleiman 23 June 1957
Anne Frank Stichting
Anne Frank Stichting
Letter Amstelodamum to the city quoted in:
MJ Rijnders, gesch. AFS o.4
Jo Kleiman in a letter to Otto, 2 December 1956
Otto's quote from a clipping about the scale-model,
24 May 1962, newspaper unknown
Archief Anne Frank Stichting
Het Achterhuis, 15 juli 1944

Note:
The bibliography and the quotation index contained
in this appendix essentially refer to the original
(Dutch) version of the museum catalogue.
The reader is advised to consult the following books
for some of the sources used in preparing the
English translation:
Anne Frank, The Diary of a Young Girl – The
Definitive Edition, edited by Otto H. Frank and
Mirjam Pressler - Doubleday, New York 1995.
The Diary of Anne Frank – The Critical Edition,
prepared by the Netherlands State Institute for War
Documentation – Doubleday, New York 1989.
Anne Frank's Tales from the Secret Annex – Stories,
essays, fables and reminiscences written in hiding –
Doubleday, New York 1983.
Anne Frank Remembered – The Story of the
Woman Who Helped to Hide the Frank Family,
Miep Gies with Alison Leslie Gold – Simon and
Schuster 1987.
Roses from the Earth: The Biography of Anne Frank
1929-1945, Carol Anne Lee – Penguin U.K. 1998.

Pen Names

When Anne Frank rewrites her diary with the idea
of publishing it, she creates a pseudonym for all the
central characters. Otto Frank chooses to retain part
of these pen names in the 1947 publication of the diary.
In the Critical Edition of 1985 all the actual names are
published. In the new version of the diary published in
1991 some of the people in hiding still have pen names,
but the helpers once again have their real names.
In this catalogue everyone is referred to by their
actual name.

Actual Name	Pen Name
Anne Frank	Anne Frank
Margot Frank	Margot Frank
Otto Frank ('Pim')	Otto Frank
Edith Frank	Edith Frank
Hermann van Pels	Mr. Van Daan
Auguste van Pels	Mrs. Van Daan
Peter van Pels	Peter van Daan
Fritz Pfeffer	Mr. Dussel
Jo Kleiman	Mr. Koophuis
Victor Kugler	Mr. Kraler
Bep Voskuijl	Elli Vossen
Johan Voskuijl	Mr. Vossen
Miep Gies	Miep van Santen
Jan Gies	Henk van Santen

Photography Credits

Abbreviations

AB	Allard Bovenberg, Amsterdam
AFF	Anne Frank Fonds, Bazel
AFS	Anne Frank Stichting, Amsterdam
AKG	Archiv für Kunst und Geschichte, Berlin
AN	Arnold Newman
ANP	ANP Foto, Den Haag
AR	Nationaal Archief, Den Haag
AVi	Aviodome luchtfotografie, Lelystad
BA	Bundesarchiv, Koblenz
BPK	Bildarchiv Preussischer Kulturbesitz, Berlin
BR	M. Chagall, Anne Frank, c/o Beeldrecht Amsterdam 2004
CF	20th Century Fox Home Entertainment
CS	Caroline Schröder
Coll.vB	Van Beusekom Collection
Coll.V	Visser Collection
Coll.D	Deliema Collection
Coll.G	Gies Collection
Coll.S	Schloss Collection
Coll.Si	Silverberg Collection
Coll.So	Souget Collection
Coll.St	Stanfield Collection
Coll.vW	Van Wijk Collection
Coll.W	Wijnberg Collection
Coll.dW	De Winter Collection
DS	Dineke Stam
EvZ	Egbert van Zon
GA	Gemeentearchief, Amsterdam
GB	Gon Buurman
GBW	Galerie Bilderwelt, Reinhard Schultz, Berlin
GD	Gedenkstätte Dachau, München
GL	Gerechtelijk Laboratorium, Den Haag
GN	Gedenkstätte Neuengamme
HNP	Harry Naeff Pressebilder, Zürich
IS	Institut für Stadtgeschichte, Frankfurt am Main
IWM	Imperial War Museum, London
JH	Juul Hondius
KB	Karel Bönnekamp
LH	Linda Hirsch
MA	Maria Austria Instituut, Amsterdam
MDR	Museum of the Danish Resistance, 1940-1945
ME	Marie Ellifritz
MJR	Marie-José Rijnders
MV	Maarten van de Velde
NA	National Archives, Washington DC
NFM	Violette Cornelius/Nederlands Fotomuseum, Rotterdam
NRK	Informatiebureau Nederlandse Rode Kruis, coll. Oorlogsarchief
NIOD	Nederlands Instituut voor Oorlogsdocumentatie, Amsterdam
PC	Private Collection
PL	P. Lust
PMO	Panstwowe Muzeum Oswiecim
SF	Spaarnestad Fotoarchief
SO	Sovfoto/Eastfoto, New York
TMM	Terezin Memorial Museum
USHMM	United States Holocaust Memorial Museum, Washington DC
VM	Verzetsmuseum Amsterdam
W	Erven H.J. Wijnne
WB	Herinneringscentrum Kamp Westerbork, Westerbork
YV	Yad Vashem, Jeruzalem
Yivo	Yivo Institute for Jewish Research, New York

The blue p indicated in the photo credits applies to the small portrait photos at the top of various pages of this book.
Some of the photographs used in this publication have origins that cannot be traced with certainty. Those who discover their own photos here may contact the Anne Frank House.

page 2	AFF/AFS	
10	1 AFF/AFS	
12	2 PC/Fraifeld	
	3 AFF/AFS	
	p AFF/AFS	
	IS	
	BPK	
14	4 AFF/AFS	
	5 AFF/AFS	
	6 PC/Fraifeld	
	p AFF/AFS	
	BPK	
	AFS	
16	7 AFF/AFS	
	8 AFF/AFS	
	9 AFF/AFS	
	p AFF/AFS	
	AKG	
	NIOD	
18	10 AFF/AFS	
19	11 AFF/AFS	
20	12 AFF/AFS	
	13 AFF/AFS	
	14 AFS (AB)	
	p AFF/AFS	
	NIOD	
	IS	
22	15 AFS/Coll.vB	
	16 AFS (AB)	
	17 AFF/AFS	
	p AFS/Coll.V	
	BA	
	NIOD	
24	18 AFF/AFS	
	19 AFF/AFS	
	20 PC	
	p PC/v.Creveld	
	NIOD	
	NIOD	
25	21 AFF/AFS	
23	22 AFF/AFS	
	23 AFF/AFS	
	24 AFS	
	p AFS	
	BPK	
	NIOD	
30	25 AFF/AFS	
	26 AFF/AFS	
	27 AFF/AFS	
	p AFF/AFS	
	BPK	
	SF	
32	28 AFF/AFS	
	29 AFF/AFS	
	30 AFS/Coll.G	
	p AFS/Coll.G	
		NIOD
		AFS (AB)
34	31	AFS/Coll.G
36	32	AFS (AB)
	33	AFS (AB)
	34	AFF/AFS
	35	AFF/AFS
	p	AFS (GB)
		BPK
		BPK
38	36	AFF/AFS
	37	KLM
	38	AFS/Coll.S
	p	AFS/Coll.Si
		VM
		NIOD (A. Wijnberg
40	39	MA
	40	MA
	42	AFF/AFS
		AFS/Coll.V
	43	AFS
		AFS
	48	AFS (AB)
	50	1 MA
		2 MA
		3 AFS (AB)
		4 AFS (AB)
		5 AFS (AB)
	52	1 MA
		2 AFS (AB)
		3 AFS (AB)
		4 AFS (PL)
		5 AFS/Coll.W
		p AFS (GB)
	54	1 AFS (AB)
		2 MA
		3 MA
		p AFS
	56	1 AFS (AB)
		2 AFS
		3 AFS (AB)
		4 MA
		5 AFS (AB)
	60	AFS (AB)
	62	1 MA
		2 AFS (AB)
		3 AFS (AB)
	64	MA
	65	AFS (AB)
	66	1 AFS (AB)
		2 MA
		3 AFS (AB)
	70	AFS (AB)
	72	1 AFS (AB)
		2 AFS (AB)
		3 AFS (AB)

Publication and Production Anne Frank House,
Anneke Boekhoudt, Nico de Bruijn, Mieke Sobering
Compilation and Editing Anne Frank House,
Menno Metselaar, Ruud van der Rol, Dineke Stam
Final Editing Hansje Galesloot
Photo Archive Anne Frank House, Yt Stoker
Illustration Eric van Rootselaar
Corrections Miriam Gerretzen
Translation Epicycles/Amsterdam, Lorraine T. Miller
Design Beukers Scholma/Haarlem
Jacket and Case Design Yellowstone Ltd.
Lithography Graphic Production Bureau, Lia Durrer
With Thanks to J.J. van Borssum Waalkes, Max van
Creveld, Sally Deliema, Buddy Elias, Ed Fraifeld,
Henry Giersthove, Miep Gies, Paul Gies, Stef van Hoeve,
Gertrud Naumann, Arnold Newman, Jacqueline Sanders,
Eva Schloss, Edmond Silverberg, Sonja Souget,
W.F. van Tellingen, Marijke Witsel, M. Wijnne-Rouma

Refurnishing Museum Anne Frank House,
Wouter van der Sluis, Gerrit Netten
Acquisitions Refurnishing David Peters, NOB Props,
Rein van der Pol
Photographs Refurnishing Allard Bovenberg

This edition published in 2004 by Overlook Duckworth,
Peter Mayer Publishers, Inc. New York, Woodstock,
and London

New York
141 Wooster Street
New York, NY 10012

Woodstock
One Overlook Drive
Woodstock, NY 12498
www.overlookpress.com
[For individual orders, bulk and special sales, contact
our Woodstock office]

London
90-93 Cowcross Street
London EC1M 6BF
inquiries@duckworth-publishers.co.uk
www.ducknet.co.uk

A CIP record for this book is available from the Library
of Congress and the British Library

Printed and bound in China

9 8 7 6 5 4 3 2 1
ISBN 1-58567-628-4 (US)
ISBN 0-7156-3329-5 (UK)

Anne Frank House
Prinsengracht 263, Amsterdam
P.O. Box 730, 1000 AS Amsterdam
The Netherlands
www.annefrank.nl